Knit Your **Socks** on Straight

A New and Inventive Technique with Just Two Needles

ALICE CURTIS

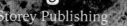

Storey Publishing

The mission of Storey Publishing is to serve our customers by
publishing practical information that encourages
personal independence in harmony with the environment.

Edited by Pam Thompson and Gwen Steege
Art direction and book design by Mary Winkelman Velgos

Cover photography by © Geneve Hoffman Photography,
    except knitting needles by © John Polak Photography
Interior photography by © Geneve Hoffman Photography, 1, 11, 25, 26, 31, 32, 35, 37, 39 (inset), 40, 41, 44, 45,
    49, 51, 54, 57, 59, 60, 62, 67, 68, 73, 75, 77, 80, 83, 85, 87, 91, 95, 97, 103, 106, 109, 113, 116, 117, 121, 125, 128, 131,
    135, and 138; © John Polak Photography, 4–10, 12–22, 29, 34, 39 (needles), 43, 48, 53, 58, 65, 70–72, 79, 84,
    89, 96, 105, 111, 120, 127, and 133; and Mars Vilaubi, 23
Set design by Geneve Hoffman
Styling by Wendy Freedman
Charts created by Charlotte Quiggle and Alice Curtis and drawn by Missy Shepler
    How-to illustrations by Alison Kolesar

Indexed by Christine R. Lindemer, Boston Road Communications

© 2013 by Alice Curtis

Storey Publishing
210 MASS MoCA Way
North Adams, MA 01247
www.storey.com

Printed in China by Toppan Leefung Printing Ltd.
10 9 8 7 6 5 4 3 2 1

Library of Congress Cataloging-in-Publication Data

Curtis, Alice.
  Knit your socks on straight / by Alice Curtis.
    pages cm
  Includes index.
  ISBN 978-1-61212-008-9 (hardcover with concealed wire-o : alk. paper)
  ISBN 978-1-60342-910-8 (ebook)
  1. Knitting—Patterns. 2. Socks. I. Title.
TT825.C875 2013
746.43'2—dc23
                        2012042978

To my father, Eric Walter Eliasson, who instilled a love for books and reading at an early age and encouraged me in any and all of my needlework interests.

To my husband, Jim, for being my support and putting up with me working into the wee hours of the night many times.

And to my class of intrepid beginner knitters, without whom this book would not have been.

Contents

4

ONE OF MY EARLIEST memories is of carefully threading a shoelace through the holes in a stiff card to outline a colorful picture. Since then, embroidery, sewing, and yarn crafts have been a source of entertainment and comfort throughout my life. Part of the fun lies in shopping to pick out new materials to play with: the crisp new fabric, the smooth hanks of embroidery thread, and the skeins of soft, squishy yarn in all the colors of the rainbow.

Eventually I learned enough to begin to share my experience and knowledge with others. Whenever I hear the wistful cry, "I wish I could do that," I'm happy to say, "Let me show you how!" The sense of satisfaction that comes from enabling another fiber lover to master a skill is second to none.

As a yarn shop owner, I encouraged lots of experimentation. Knitting and crochet are for slowing down and taking a break from the hectic pace of our busy lives — and for playing! I believe strongly that there is no one right way to do things, as long as it looks the way you want it to and the project gets finished. That should be the goal: to have a finished project, yes, but especially to have fun while you're making it.

In the process of teaching beginning knitters, the subject of socks came up, and everyone clamored to make them. They were interested and enthusiastic, but I had a dilemma. They were emphatic about not wanting to tackle double-pointed needles. Socks are almost always knitted in the round — what was I to do? I looked at patterns for easy two-needle socks that could be knitted flat, and I tried several. The results were nothing I would ever want to wear! They neither looked nor felt good. Most often the seam went down the back of the leg and heel and under the foot. One even involved a complicated seaming plan that placed a seam sideways across the top of the heel. Ouch! It really hurt. There was no choice: I had to design something that my students would be proud to wear. Well, the class was a success. We had fun, and they each went home with a pair of socks.

I continued looking for patterns for simple, flat-knitted socks for my shop and was disappointed to find that few books or patterns (aside from some reprints of vintage booklets) even mentioned two-needle socks. When they did, the terminology and supplies were outdated. I find that old instructions assume knitters possess certain skills. They do not explain how to seam the sock so it is flat and comfortable. And if the seams are flat, they are still quite visible. Patterns for two-needle socks can be found occasionally on the Internet, but they are often extremely plain, and unless you are willing to take the time for skillful seaming, they are not comfortable, and the seams are obvious and unsightly. Flat seaming is a skill that does not appeal to most of today's knitters, due to the time and patience it requires.

In short, I was left with the impression that two-needle socks are a make-do, work-around solution for second-rate socks. But this does not have to be the case! Knitting socks on straight needles is a viable design alternative. I developed new designs for socks that are easy to knit, comfortable to wear, and attractive to the eye.

Here they are! The more I knitted, the more fun I was having coming up with new ideas, which is why, you may notice, all the socks have leisure-time themes, starting out with Jelly Beans (page 24) and winding up at Carnegie Hall (page 133). All the socks are knitted flat on straight needles (or going back and forth on circulars, as if they were straight). These patterns range from very basic beginner socks to more advanced. My only design criterion was to knit them flat. This took some creative thinking, but the result is socks that are satisfying both to knit and to wear.

If you feel that you have been missing out on sock knitting because double-pointed needles seem fiddly or intimidating — or you just prefer to use straight needles — you are not alone. Using my seam technique, there is no sewing involved, and the seam is an integral, flexible part of the fabric of the sock. The seam is easy to do and fairly quick to finish. All patterns are carefully planned to integrate the seam into the overall design. The finished sock comes off the needles and onto the foot with the same joy and comfort as a traditionally knitted sock.

THIS BOOK was written specifically for those who like and prefer to use straight needles. All the patterns are knit on only straight needles. They are knitted from the top down, meaning that they start with the cuff and end at the toe. The leg is knitted to a length specified by the pattern and then the heel is worked. The heel is generally worked on half the stitches of the sock.

Because these patterns are knitted flat there is a seam. (Obviously!) I have located the seam most often on the side of the leg and foot, which results in a right and a left sock. Since the heel flap is usually not centered, the number of unworked instep stitches on each side of the heel flap is different. These instep stitches may be placed on waste yarn or a stitch holder while working on the heel, or simply held in reserve on the needles. After the heel is knitted and the gusset brings the stitch count back to the original number of stitches, the foot is knitted. The pattern suggests a length, but it

TIP

When I bring my knitting with me, I often use circular needles, even if I'm knitting flat. This prevents me from misplacing a needle and makes it easy to stuff my knitting into my bag without breaking or bending my needles. I like to use a 24-inch circular because the needle tips are a little longer and easier to hold.

is a good idea to fit them according to the intended wearer's foot. The sock is then finished with the toe.

Swatching

Every pattern contains information about the yarn and needles I used to knit them. Do not be tempted to assume that if you replicate that you'll get the same results I did. Make a swatch at least 30 stitches wide and 4 inches long, in either stockinette stitch or the stitch pattern used in the sock. Consider this a warm-up exercise before getting into the actual knitting. Wash as you would wash your socks and let it dry. Use a gauge ruler to measure across the stitches and up and down the rows. Jot these numbers down and compare them to the pattern. Try to get as close as possible to the pattern gauge. It is important to knit a swatch in your yarn, especially if you are substituting a different yarn, to check what your personal tension is with your needles. You may need to change the size of the needles you are using to get a smaller or larger stitch and row count. Otherwise your finished project may not be the right size. You can also choose to purposefully knit with different yarn and needles to obtain a different size than the pattern offers. Some experience is needed for this, but if you are comfortable with some math to ensure you get the desired size, then go for it!

Casting On

I like to cast on while holding both needles in one hand and using them as one. This gives me nice, evenly sized, bigger stitches, without trying too hard to cast on loosely. It always makes knitting that first row much easier. If you have a needle several sizes larger, you could use that for the cast on instead. My favorite cast on is the long-tail (also called Continental), because it makes a nice sturdy edge for the top of your sock and yet is fairly elastic. No one likes to wear a sock that cuts in at the ankle. Socks that are too tight at the top never get worn. Don't let that happen to yours!

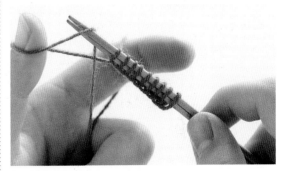

Casting on

Pull out a length of yarn (about a yard for most of the sock patterns) and make a slip knot. Put this on over the two knitting needles held together and make it snug. Keep the tail end close and the working yarn away from your body, and hold the needles in your right hand with the points facing left. Hold both lengths of yarn in your left hand with the last

Round heel

Short-row heel

three fingers. Put your thumb and forefinger between the yarn and spread to make a triangular, slingshot shape. Keep fairly close to the needles, about 2 inches away. Now turn your left hand up so the palm faces up to the ceiling. The yarn wrapped around the thumb will look like an X on your hand. Put the tips of the needles under the X and swing over toward your forefinger, go over the yarn, and without letting it slip, swing back to

your thumb and back under the X. Now snug the stitch up to the needles. Repeat to cast on as many stitches as directed by the pattern.

Heels

I have used two popular heel options that are found in most basic knitting books.

The *round heel* is the most commonly used and the easiest to learn. Most of the patterns in this book use this heel

TIP

When picking up the stitches on the side of the heel flap, knit an extra stitch into the stitch in the row just below the heel flap, then finish the row. On the next row, work the last instep stitch together with this extra stitch to prevent a gap between gusset and leg stitches.

method, with a couple variations for the heel flap. Basically a round heel begins with what is called a heel flap knitted on half the stitches of the sock. Whatever that number is, that is how many rows you knit. Then a series of short rows turn the heel and shape it to fit around your heel. (Short rows are simply that; rows that are stopped short and the work turned. This builds height into a specific area for shaping.) Stitches are picked up along the sides of the flap, generally half the number of rows knitted. You will have many more stitches than you started with across the row, so you need the gusset decreases to bring you back to the original stitch count.

The gusset can be placed at any point on the heel flap; it still does the job of decreasing the stitches around the foot.

The *short-row heel* is more similar to a store-bought sock and smoother on the back of the heel. It takes a bit more patience, but is not too difficult to

PICKING UP STITCHES FOR THE GUSSET

Here's what it looks like to pick up the heel-flap stitches when you're making a classic round heel. In a classic stockinette-stitch sock, on one side of the heel flap you pick up knit stitches and on the other side of the flap, purl stitches.

Picking up knit stitches (American)

Picking up purl stitches (American)

Picking up knit stitches (Continental)

Picking up purl stitches (Continental)

master. Again, the heel is knitted on half the stitches. The heel is shaped by knitting short rows of decreasing length back and forth until only about an inch of active knitting is left. At this point, short rows of increasing length are worked until all the stitches are incorporated back into the knitting, creating a cup for the heel to fit in. Knitting across the entire sock then continues.

Toes

Most sock patterns today use a *wedge toe*, similar to that of Touch Me Not (page 127) and Carnegie Hall (page 133), but I have found that the *star toe* and the *round toe* work best for most of these sock patterns. First, they are easy to finish — there's no Kitchener stitch! Also, both of these toes easily accommodate the seam.

The *star toe* divides the toe stitches into four equal sections, and each section is decreased by 1 stitch on right-side rows until about half the stitch count remains. Then decreases are worked on both right- and wrong-side rows until only 8 stitches remain. The yarn is cut long enough to use for the seam (five or six times the length of the sock), threaded through all the stitches using a yarn needle, and pulled tight to close the toe.

My *round toe* is a variation on the traditional version, with the same number of rows, but the decrease rows are reorganized slightly to keep the decreases on the right side. The toe stitches are divided into equal sections, and decreased 1 stitch for each section. Then a number of stockinette rows are worked before the next decrease row. When decreased to the final stitch count as specified by the pattern, the yarn is cut long enough to use for the seam (five or six times the length of the sock), threaded through all the stitches using a yarn needle, and pulled tight to close the toe. See, no Kitchener stitch!

That being said, Kitchener stitch (page 141) is used to finish the cuff of the Livin' in Blue Jeans (page 71) socks. And it is a useful skill to learn.

Wedge toe

Star toe

Round toe

THE KEY TO these socks lies in making a beautiful seam that blends into and becomes a part of the design of the sock. To make beautiful seams, you have to start with beautiful edges.

To keep the edge stitches properly oriented, the first stitch of each row must be slipped purlwise — simply moving the stitch from the left needle to the right needle without turning it; and with the working yarn in front for a purl stitch or in back for a knit stitch. In other words, if the last stitch of the preceding row was a knit stitch, your first stitch will look like a purl. In that case, you would keep your working yarn in front as you slip and then transfer the yarn to the back or keep it in front to continue working as the pattern requires.

Take some care with this! It's easy to forget and work the stitch instead of slipping it, or to wrap the yarn around the outside of the slipped stitch instead of having it go where it needs to go *after* the first stitch is slipped.

Watch where you hold the yarn.

Slipping a knit stitch purlwise

Slipping a purl stitch purlwise

It's easy to do, but just as easy to forget.

This edge (left) shows what happens if you forget to slip the stitch or if you wrap the yarn.

What you want is an edge that looks like this one: a perfect chain.

Closing the Seam

Since these seams are so important in the design and fit of the sock, you need to make them as smooth as possible. I found that a crocheted seam does the trick. I used to close the seam with my knitting needles, picking up and binding off the stitches at the same time, creating a seam similar to that of a three-needle bind off. This, I realized, was exactly the same as a crocheted slip stitch — but harder. I switched to using a crochet hook; it is *so* much easier to handle the sock in one hand and the hook in the other.

You won't be surprised to hear that using the appropriate-size crochet hook is critical to a flexible, smooth seam. Choose a hook large enough to keep the seam stitches the same size as the slipped stitches along the edge. You may need to experiment. Generally, use the biggest size hook that you can get through the slipped stitch.

Having chosen a hook, fold the sock with wrong sides together, and carefully match up the slipped stitches by pinning the edges together every couple inches with seaming pins or the ubiquitous T-pins from the top down to keep the stitches aligned. This may take a couple minutes, but it's more than worth it. Think of the time you'll save by not having to rip out and try again when things go awry!

Starting at the toe where the stitches are pulled together tightly and working from right to left, insert the hook through two matching slipped stitches and pull a loop through. Moving to the next set of matching slipped stitches, pull another loop through and then through the loop on the hook.

Pin carefully.

Work it all the way up the sock to the last 2 matching stitches. Then pull the remaining yarn through the last loop. Weave the ends of the yarn into your work, and you are finished.

For the really persnickety knitter, the directions for seaming call for stitching from the back or the front of the seam, depending on whether you're knitting the right or left sock. Paying attention to this detail will give you perfectly symmetrical socks. It's also fine to work them both the same, which reminds me: I designated left and right socks for clarity in the instructions. But wear them however you like! My daughter prefers to wear the seams on the inside of her foot; I prefer them on the outside.

My way is not necessarily the right way to finish this seam. The same effect may be accomplished with a knitted bind off or even a chain stitch as worked in embroidery. Just remember to keep the finishing stitches the same size as the slipped stitches along the edges.

It is certainly possible to use a running stitch to sew the seam, but there

TROUBLESHOOTING

If you missed slipping a stitch somewhere along the way and knitted one instead, you will see two edge stitches that are smaller than all the others, throwing off the matching stitches. Just skip one of those stitches and continue on as usual. The goal is to end up with the last two matching stitches stitched together.

are distinct disadvantages to this, the first being a lack of flexibility and lengthwise stretch compared with the rest of the sock. Also, the seam tends to look zigzagged, making it stand out against the rest of the knitting. As far as a typical sewn seam is concerned, a backstitch would offer a more flexible straight seam, but the overlapping stitches may be too visible. Still, as I have said, the goal here is to accomplish a finished object, so if you are happy with the results of your chosen seam, then use it.

Working the crocheted slip stitch from the front ...

and from the back of the seam

Play!

Try things out. Experiment and ask questions. If it doesn't work, rip it out. It's okay — it means you learned something. Try something else. Remember that I invented these patterns with fun and leisure in mind. Envision yourself sipping another cappuccino in your frothy lace Coffee Break socks (page 105), or running errands in Flip-Flops in February (page 34). How about listening to an opera and sipping wine in Carnegie Hall socks (page 133) or baking cookies after sledding in Gingerbread Men and Snowmen socks (page 111)? I would love to see what you come up with. I'll be watching on Ravelry.

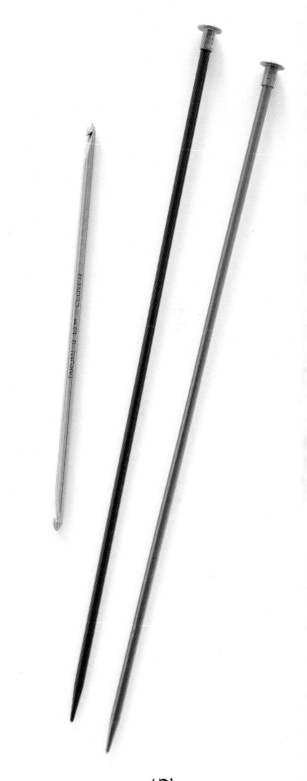

The last two stitches

BASIC WORSTED-WEIGHT socks knit up quickly and are the perfect first sock project. Try these socks first, and you'll be ready to take on any straight-needle sock!

Pattern Notes

- This sock is designed with a round heel and star toe.
- Don't forget to slip the first stitch of every row purlwise. This is vital to achieving a smooth seam.

SIZES	Woman S (M, L)
FINISHED MEASUREMENTS	Leg circumference: 7½ (8, 8¾)" Foot length: 8 (9, 10)"
YARN	Patons Classic Wool, worsted, 100% wool, 210 yds / 100 g, 1 skein Worn Denim 77117
NEEDLES	US 6 (4.0 mm) 9" straight needles *or size needed to obtain gauge*
OTHER SUPPLIES	Waste yarn, small stitch holders, or split-ring markers; two stitch markers; seaming pins; yarn needle; US H/8 (5.0 mm) crochet hook *or size needed to match the slipped edge stitches* (see Closing the Seam, page 15)
GAUGE	20 stitches and 28 rows = 4" in stockinette stitch Knit a swatch for accurate sizing.

Left Sock

CUFF

Knitting the cuff

Cast on 37 (41, 45) stitches loosely.

Row 1 (RS) Slip 1, *p1, k1; repeat from * to end.

Slipping the first stitch of every row, work 13 more rows in established rib.

Row 15 (RS) Slipping the first stitch, knit across, decreasing 1 stitch in the middle of the row — 36 (40, 44) stitches.

Rows 16–18 Slipping the first stitch of every row, work 13 more rows in stockinette stitch.

HEEL FLAP

Heels are worked on half the stitches of the sock. Although the rest of the stitches (the instep) may be left on the needle and not worked, it may be easier to place them on waste yarn or stitch

Working the heel flap

holders until the heel is finished and you are ready to put the instep stitches back on the needle. The rows dividing the heel stitches and the instep stitches are worked slightly differently for the left and right socks to ensure the correct placement of the seams.

Row 1 (RS) Slip 1, k1, transfer these 2 stitches to waste yarn, a small stitch holder, or a split-ring marker; [slip 1, k1] 9 (10, 11) times, turn; transfer remaining 16 (18, 20) stitches to waste yarn or another small stitch holder — 18 (20, 22) flap stitches.

Row 2 (WS) Slip 1, p17 (19, 21), turn.

Working on the flap stitches only, repeat [Rows 1 and 2] 8 (9, 10) times — 18 (20, 22) flap rows.

Look at the sides of the heel flap for the longer stitches; you may have to roll the edge out to see them clearly. Count 9 (10, 11) long stitches. These are the slipped stitches — you will use them later when picking up stitches for the gusset.

HEEL TURN

Turning the heel

Row 1 (RS) Slip 1, k10 (10, 12), ssk, k1, turn, leaving 4 (6, 6) stitches unworked.

Row 2 (WS) Slip 1, p5 (3, 5), p2tog, p1, turn, leaving 4 (6, 6) stitches unworked.

Row 3 Slip 1, knit to 1 stitch before gap formed on previous row, ssk [1 stitch from each side of the gap], k1, turn.

Row 4 Slip 1, purl to 1 stitch before gap formed on previous row, p2tog [1 stitch from each side of gap], p1, turn.

Repeat Rows 3 and 4 until all heel stitches have been worked, ending with a WS row — 12 (12, 14) heel stitches remain.

GUSSET

Stitches picked up for working the gusset

See page 10 for picking up the slip stitches along the edge of the heel flap.

Row 1 (RS) Knit to the end of the heel, then pick up and knit 9 (10, 11) stitches in the long slipped stitches along the side of the flap, place marker; k16 (18, 20) from holder.

Row 2 (WS) Slip 1, purl to end of heel; pick up and purl [from the back of the stitch] 9 (10, 11) stitches in the long slipped stitches along the side of the flap, place marker; p2 from holder — 48 (52, 58) stitches.

Row 3 Slip 1, knit to marker, k1, ssk, knit to 3 stitches before next marker, k2tog, k1, knit to end — 46 (50, 56) stitches.

Row 4 Slip 1, purl to end.

Repeat [Rows 3 and 4] 5 (5, 6) times — 36 (40, 44) stitches.

Remove markers.

Gussets complete

FOOT

Knitting the foot

Slipping the first stitch of every row, work even in stockinette stitch until foot measures about 6 (7, 8)" from the back of the heel, or 2" shorter than desired length.

STAR TOE

Finishing the toe

The toe is divided into four equal quadrants. The stitch count in each quadrant is decreased on RS rows until about half the stitches remain, then decreases are worked on both RS and WS rows until 8 stitches remain, ending with a WS row.

Setup Row (RS) Slip 1, k6 (7, 9), k2tog, place marker, *k7 (8, 10), k2tog, place marker, repeat from * to end — 32 (36, 40) stitches.

Row 2 Slip 1, purl to end.

Row 3 (RS Decrease Row) Slipping the first stitch, *knit to 2 stitches before marker, k2tog; repeat from * to end — 28 (32, 36) stitches.

Repeat [Rows 2 and 3] 2 (3, 3) times — 20 (20, 24) stitches.

Next Row (WS Decrease Row) Slip 1, ssp, purl to marker, *p2tog, purl to marker; repeat from * to end — 16 (16, 20) stitches.

Repeat RS and WS Decrease Rows until 8 stitches remain, ending with a WS row.

Measure the yarn out to about five times the length of sock and cut. Using a yarn needle, thread the tail through all stitches and pull tight. Do not cut the yarn yet; the rest is used for seaming.

SEAM

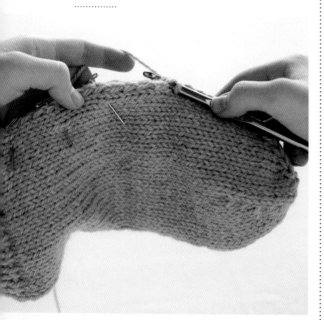

Working the seam

Fold the sock with wrong sides together. Match up the slipped edge stitches and pin in place. Using the crochet hook, slip stitch knitwise from the front into each corresponding set of stitches up to the top of the cuff to close the seam. (See page 15.)

Fasten off. Weave in ends. Block as desired.

Right Sock

Work as for Left Sock to Heel Flap.

HEEL FLAP

Row 1 (RS) Slip 1, k15 (17, 19) then transfer these stitches to waste yarn or a small stitch holder; [slip 1, k1] 9 (10, 11) times, turn; transfer remaining 2 stitches to waste yarn, another small stitch holder, or a split-ring marker — 18 (20, 22) flap stitches.

Row 2 Slip 1, purl 17 (19, 21), turn.

Complete Heel Flap and Heel Turn as for Left Sock.

GUSSET

Row 1 (RS) Knit to end of heel; pick up and knit 9 (10, 11) stitches along the side of the flap, place marker; k2 from holder.

Row 2 Slip 1, purl to the end of the heel; pick up and purl [from the back of the stitch] 9 (10, 11) stitches along the side of the flap, place marker; p16 (18, 20) from holder — 48 (52, 58) stitches.

Continue as for Left Sock until Star Toe is complete.

SEAM

Work as for Left Sock, but slip stitch purlwise from the back to close the seam.

Jelly Beans

Americans have a love affair with sweets, and nothing evokes fun and giggles like jelly beans from a candy shop. Bright, cheerful sport-weight socks knit in easy-care washable yarn are sure to lift your spirits. These are shown knit in two lengths for little feet.

SIZES	Child S (M, L)
FINISHED MEASUREMENTS	Circumference: 5 (6, 7¼)" Foot length: 5½ (6, 7)"
YARN	Universal Yarns Uptown Baby Sport, sport weight, 100% acrylic, 361 yds / 100 g, 1 skein Petal #209 (crew sock) or 1 skein Violet #214 (kneesock)
NEEDLES	US 4 (3.5 mm) 9" straight needles *or size needed to obtain gauge*
OTHER SUPPLIES	Two stitch markers, waste yarn or small stitch holders, yarn needle, seaming pins, US G/6 (4.25 mm) crochet hook *or size needed to match the slipped edge stitches* (see Closing the Seam, page 15)
GAUGE	24 stitches and 32 rows = 4" in stockinette stitch Knit a swatch for accurate sizing.

Left Sock

Kneesock

CUFF

Cast on 37 (45, 53) stitches loosely.

Row 1 (RS) Slip 1, *p1, k1; repeat to end.

Slipping the first stitch of every row, work 9 (11, 13) more rows in established rib.

LEG

Row 1 (RS) Slip 1, knit to end, increasing 3 stitches evenly across row, turn — 40 (48, 56) stitches.

Work 9 (11 13) rows in stockinette stitch.

Decrease Row (RS) Slip 1, k12 (15, 18), k2tog, place marker, ssk, knit to end — 38 (46, 54) stitches.

Continuing in stockinette stitch, repeat Decrease Row every 10th (14th, 16th) row 3 more times — 32 (44, 48) stitches.

Work even until sock measures 7½ (8¾, 10)" or desired length.

Crew Sock

CUFF

Cast on 33 (41, 49) stitches loosely.

Row 1 (RS) Slip 1, *p1, k1; repeat to end.

Slipping the first stitch of every row, work 9 (11, 13) more rows in established rib.

LEG

Decreasing 1 stitch (k2tog) in the middle of the first row, work in stockinette stitch until sock measures 3 (5, 6)" or desired length — 32 (40, 48) stitches.

Both Versions

HEEL FLAP

Row 1 (RS) Slip 1, k1, transfer these 2 stitches to waste yarn or a small stitch holder; [slip 1, k1] 8 (10, 12) times, turn; transfer remaining 14 (18, 22) stitches to waste yarn or another small stitch holder — 16 (20, 24) flap stitches.

Row 2 Slip 1, p15 (19, 23), turn.

Working flap stitches only, repeat [Rows 1 and 2] 7 (9, 11) times — 16 (20, 24) flap rows.

HEEL TURN

Row 1 (RS) Slip 1, k8 (10, 12), ssk, k1, turn, leaving 4 (6, 8) stitches unworked.

Row 2 (WS) Slip 1, p3, p2tog, p1, turn, leaving 4 (6, 8) stitches unworked.

Row 3 Slip 1, knit to 1 stitch before gap formed on previous row, ssk [1 stitch from each side of gap], k1, turn.

Row 4 Slip 1, purl to 1 stitch before gap formed on previous row, p2tog [1 stitch from each side of gap], p1, turn.

Repeat Rows 3 and 4 until all heel stitches have been worked, ending with a WS row — 10 (12, 14) heel stitches remain.

GUSSET

Row 1 Knit to the end of the heel; pick up and knit 8 (10, 12) stitches along the side of the flap, place marker; k14 (18, 22) stitches from holder.

Row 2 Slip 1, purl to end of heel; pick up and purl [from the back of the stitch] 8 (10, 12) stitches along the side of the flap, place marker; p2 stitches from holder — 42 (52, 62) stitches.

Row 3 Slip 1, knit to marker, k1, ssk, knit to 3 stitches before next marker, k2tog, k1, knit to end — 40 (50, 60) stitches.

Row 4 Slip 1, purl to end.

Repeat [Rows 3 and 4] 4 (5, 6) times — 32 (40, 48) stitches. Remove markers.

FOOT

Slipping the first stitch of every row, work even in stockinette stitch until foot measures about 3¾ (4¼, 4¾)" from the back of the heel, or about 1½" shorter than desired length.

STAR TOE

Setup Row (RS) Slip 1, k5 (7, 9), k2tog, place marker, *k6 (8, 10), k2tog, place marker; repeat from * to end, turn — 28 (36, 44) stitches.

Row 2 Slip 1, purl to end.

Row 3 (RS Decrease Row) Slipping the first stitch, *knit to 2 stitches before marker, k2tog; repeat from * to end, turn — 24 (32, 36) stitches.

Repeat [Rows 2 and 3] 2 (3, 3) times — 20 (20, 24) stitches.

Next Row (WS Decrease Row) Slip 1, ssp, purl to marker, *p2tog, purl to marker; repeat from * to end, turn — 16 (16, 20) stitches.

Repeat RS and WS Decrease Rows until 8 stitches remain, working a last purl row without any decreases for size L.

27

Jelly Beans

Measure the yarn out to about five times the length of sock and cut. Using a yarn needle, thread tail through all stitches and pull up tight. Do not cut the yarn yet; the rest is used for seaming.

SEAM

Fold the sock with wrong sides together. Match up the slipped edge stitches and pin in place. Using the crochet hook, slip stitch knitwise from the front into each corresponding set of stitches up to the top of the cuff to close the seam. (See page 15).

Fasten off. Weave in ends. Block as desired.

Right Sock

Kneesock

Work Cuff and Leg as for Left Sock to Decrease Row.

Decrease Row (RS) Slip 1, k22 (27, 28), k2tog, place marker, ssk, knit to end.

Complete Leg as for Left Sock to Heel Flap.

Crew Sock

Work as for Left Sock to Heel Flap.

HEEL FLAP

Row 1 (RS) Slip 1, k13 (17, 21), transfer these stitches to waste yarn or a small stitch holder; [slip 1, k1] 8 (10, 12) times, turn; transfer remaining 2 stitches to waste yarn or another small stitch holder — 16 (20, 24) flap stitches.

Row 2 Slip 1, purl 15 (19, 23), turn.

Complete Heel Flap and Heel Turn as for Left Sock.

GUSSET

Row 1 (RS) Knit to the end of the heel; pick up and knit 8 (10, 12) stitches along the side of the flap, place marker; k2 from holder.

Row 2 Slip 1, purl to end of heel; pick up and purl [from the back of the stitch] 8 (10, 12) stitches along the side of the flap, place marker; p14 (18, 22) from holder — 42 (52, 62) stitches.

Continue as for Left Sock until Star Toe is complete.

SEAM

Work as for Left Sock, but slip stitch purlwise from the back to close the seam.

Jelly Beans

Green Leaves of Summer

These socks are named for an old song I heard on the car radio that reminded me how much time we spend outdoors in the summertime. A comfortable pair of basic stockinette socks will make your feet happy all day. Here is a classic fingering-weight sock in a smooth stockinette stitch for children and adults.

29

Pattern Notes

- This sock is designed with a round heel and star toe.
- Don't forget to slip the first stitch of every row purlwise. This is vital to achieving a smooth seam.

SIZES	Child M (Child L, Adult S, Adult M, Adult L)
FINISHED MEASUREMENTS	Circumference: 6 (7, 8, 9, 10)" Foot Length: 5¾ (6, 8¼, 9¼, 10)"
YARN	Cascade Heritage or Heritage Paints, fingering weight, 75% superwash merino wool / 25% nylon, 437 yds / 100 g, 1 skein Moss #5612 (child version) or 1 skein Celtic #9770 (adult version)
NEEDLES	US 1 (2.25 mm) 9" straight needles *or size needed to obtain gauge*
OTHER SUPPLIES	Waste yarn or small stitch holders, two stitch markers, seaming pins, US F/5 (3.75 mm) crochet hook *or size needed to match the slipped edge stitches* (see Closing the Seam, page 15)
GAUGE	32 stitches and 40 rows = 4" in stockinette stitch Knit a swatch for accurate sizing.

Left Sock

CUFF

Cast on 49 (57, 65, 73, 81) stitches loosely.

Row 1 (RS) Slip 1, *p1, k1; repeat from * to end.

Slipping the first stitch of every row, work even in established rib until piece measures 1½ (1½, 2, 2, 2)".

LEG

Decreasing 1 stitch (k2tog) in the middle of the first row, work in stockinette stitch until piece measures 4½ (5¼, 6, 8, 8)" or desired length — 48 (56, 64, 72, 80) stitches.

HEEL FLAP

Row 1 (RS) Slip 1, k1, transfer these 2 stitches to waste yarn or a small stitch holder; [slip 1, k1] 12 (14, 16, 18, 20) times, turn; transfer remaining 22 (26, 30, 35, 38) stitches to waste yarn or another small

Green Leaves of Summer

stitch holder — 24 (28, 32, 36, 40) flap stitches.

Row 2 Slip 1, p23 (27, 31, 35, 39), turn.

Working the flap stitches only, repeat [Rows 1 and 2] 11 (13, 15, 17, 19) times — 24 (28, 32, 36, 40) flap rows.

HEEL TURN

Row 1 (RS) Slip 1, k12 (14, 16, 18, 20), k2tog, k1, turn, leaving 8 (10, 12, 14, 16) stitches unworked.

Row 2 (WS) Slip 1, p3, p2tog, p1, turn, leaving 8 (10, 12, 14, 16) stitches unworked.

Row 3 Slip 1, knit to 1 stitch before gap formed on previous row, ssk [1 stitch from each side of gap], k1, turn.

Row 4 Slip 1, purl to 1 stitch before gap formed on previous row, p2tog [1 stitch from each side of gap], p1, turn.

Repeat Rows 3 and 4 until all heel stitches have been worked, ending with a WS row — 14 (16, 18, 20, 22) heel stitches remain.

GUSSET

Row 1 (RS) Knit to the end of the heel; pick up and knit 12 (14, 16, 18, 20) stitches along the side of the flap, place marker; k22 (26, 30, 35, 38) stitches from holder.

Row 2 Slip 1, purl to the end of the heel; pick up and purl [from the back of the stitch] 12 (14, 16, 18, 20) stitches along the side of the flap, place marker; p2 from holder — 62 (72, 82, 92, 102) stitches.

Row 3 Slip 1, knit to marker, k1, ssk, knit to 3 stitches before next marker, k2tog, k1, knit to end — 60 (70, 80, 90, 100) stitches.

Row 4 Slip 1, purl to end.

Repeat [Rows 3 and 4] 6 (7, 8, 9, 10) times — 48 (56, 64, 72, 80) stitches. Remove markers.

FOOT

Slipping the first stitch of every row, work even until foot measures about 4¼ (4½, 6½, 7¼, 8)" from the back of the heel, or about 1½ (1½, 1¾, 2, 2)" shorter than desired length.

STAR TOE

Setup Row (RS) Slip 1, k9 (11, 13, 15, 17), k2tog, place marker, *k10 (12, 14, 16, 18),

k2tog, place marker; repeat from * to end — 44 (52, 60, 68, 76) stitches.

Row 2 Slip 1, purl to end.

Row 3 (RS Decrease Row) Slipping the first stitch, *knit to 2 stitches before marker, k2tog; repeat from * to end — 40 (48, 56, 64, 72) stitches.

Repeat [Rows 2 and 3] 4 (6, 6, 8, 8) times — 24 (24, 32, 32, 40) stitches.

Next Row (WS Decrease Row) Slip 1, ssp, purl to marker, *p2tog, purl to marker; repeat from * to end — 20 (20, 28, 28, 36) stitches.

Repeat RS and WS Decrease Rows until 8 stitches remain, ending with a plain purl row.

Measure the yarn out to about five times the length of the sock and cut. Using a yarn needle, thread tail through all stitches and pull up tight. Do not cut the yarn yet; the rest is used for seaming.

SEAM

Fold the sock with wrong sides together. Match up the slipped edge stitches and pin in place. Using the crochet hook, slip stitch knitwise from the front into each corresponding set of stitches up to the top of the cuff to close the seam. (See page 15).

Fasten off. Weave in ends. Block as desired.

Right Sock

Work as for Left Sock to Heel Flap.

HEEL FLAP

Row 1 (RS) Slip 1, k21 (25, 29, 33, 37), transfer these stitches to waste yarn or a small stitch holder; [slip 1, k1] 12 (14, 16, 18, 20) times, turn; transfer remaining 2 stitches to waste yarn or another small stitch holder — 24 (28, 32, 36, 40) flap stitches.

Row 2 Slip 1, purl 23 (27, 31, 35, 39) stitches.

Complete Heel Flap and Heel Turn as for Left Sock.

GUSSET

Row 1 (RS) Knit to the end of the heel; pick up and knit 12 (14, 16, 18, 20) stitches along the side of the flap, place marker; k2 from holder.

Row 2 Slip 1, purl to end of heel; pick up and purl [from the back of the stitch] 12 (14, 16, 18, 20) stitches along the side of the flap, place marker; p22 (26, 30, 35, 38) stitches from holder — 62 (72, 82, 92, 102) stitches.

Continue as for Left Sock until Star Toe is complete.

SEAM

Work as for Left Sock, but slip stitch purlwise from the back to close the seam.

33

Green Leaves of Summer

Flip-Flops in February

I live in a northern climate with plenty of snow and cold temperatures. But let the sun shine and the snow melt away for a few days, and out come the flip-flops — teenage girls here are a hardy bunch! These split-toe socks are a fun way to extend the flip-flop season and still keep feet warm.

SIZES	Woman S (L)
FINISHED MEASUREMENTS	Circumference: 7 (8)" Foot length: 8 (9)"
YARN	Wisdom Yarns Marathon Sock San Francisco, fingering weight, 75% superwash wool / 25% nylon, 437 yds / 100 g, 1 skein #201
NEEDLES	US 0 (2.0 mm) 9" straight needles *or size needed to obtain gauge*
OTHER SUPPLIES	Four stitch markers, waste yarn or small stitch holder, yarn needle, US F/5 (3.75 mm) crochet hook *or size needed to match the slipped edge stitches* (see Closing the Seam, page 15)
GAUGE	36 stitches and 44 rows = 4" (10 cm) in stockinette stitch Knit a swatch for accurate sizing.

Left Sock

CUFF

Cast on 65 (73) stitches loosely.

Row 1 (RS) Slip 1, *p1, k1; repeat from * to end.

Rows 2–14 Slipping the first stitch of every row, work 13 more rows in established rib.

LEG

Decreasing 1 stitch (k2tog) in the middle of the first row, work in stockinette stitch until piece measures 3½ (4)" or desired length to heel, ending with a WS row — 64 (72) stitches.

SHORT-ROW HEEL

Setup Row (RS) Slip 1, k19 (21), place marker; work decreasing short rows on next 32 (36) stitches as follows:

Row 1 (RS) K31 (35), turn.

Row 2 (WS) Slip 1, p29 (33), turn.

Row 3 Slip 1, k28 (32), turn.

Row 4 Slip 1, p27 (31), turn.

Work 14 (16) more short rows in this fashion, working 1 fewer stitch each row and ending with a WS row that is worked as slip 1, p13 (15); turn.

Now work one more stitch in each short row until you get back to original stitch count as follows:

Row 1 (RS) Slip 1, k12, slip 1 knitwise, lift the bar between stitches and place it on the right-hand needle, then knit it together with the slipped stitch, turn.

Row 2 (RS) Slip 1, p13, slip 1 knitwise, lift the bar between stitches and place it on the right-hand needle, then purl it together with the slipped stitch, turn.

Continue working 1 more stitch each row until all heel stitches on knit (RS) row have been worked; knit to the end of the row.

Next Row (WS) Slip 1, purl across all stitches.

Flip-Flops in February

36

FOOT

Slipping the first stitch of every row, work even until the foot measures 6½" from the back of the heel, or about 2½" shorter than desired length.

TOE SETUP

Increase Row (RS) Slip 1, k38 (42), inc 1 using the e-wrap method (see page 140), place marker, k2, place marker, inc 1, k23 (27), turn — 66 (74) stitches.

Row 2 Slip 1, purl to end.

Continuing in stockinette stitch and slipping the first stitch of every row, increase by working an e-wrap before the first marker and after the second marker every RS row 3 more times, ending with a WS row; remove markers — 72 (80) stitches with 44 (48) stitches for the Main Toe Section and 28 (32) stitches for Big Toe Section.

Division Row (RS) Slip 1, k27 (31), then transfer these stitches to waste yarn or a stitch holder for the Big Toe Section; slip 1, knit to end of row.

MAIN TOE SECTION

Row 1 (WS) Slip 1, purl to end.

Row 2 (RS Decrease Row) Slip 1, k8 (9), k2tog, place marker, [k9 (10), k2tog, place marker] 3 times — 40 (44) stitches.

Slipping the first stitch of every row, decrease by working k2tog before each marker every RS row 4 (5) times — 24 stitches.

Next Row (WS Decrease Row) Slip 1, ssp, purl to marker, [p2tog, purl to marker] twice, p2tog, purl to end — 20 stitches.

Repeat RS and WS Decrease Rows until 8 stitches remain, ending with a plain purl row.

Measure the yarn out to about six times the length of the sock and cut. Using a yarn needle, thread the tail through stitches on needle and pull up tight. Do not cut the yarn yet; the rest is used for seaming.

BIG TOE

With WS facing, transfer stitches from the holder to the needle and rejoin the yarn.

37

Flip-Flops in February

Slipping the first stitch of every row, work even in stockinette stitch until the Big Toe measures 1"–1½" or desired length, ending with a WS row and decreasing 1 (2) stitch(es) (k2tog) evenly in the middle of the last row — 27 (30) stitches.

Row 1 (RS Decrease Row) Slip 1, k2tog, [k1, k2tog] 8 (9) times — 18 (20) stitches.

Row 2 Slip 1, purl to end.

Row 3 K2tog across — 9 (10) stitches.

Measure the yarn out to about 12" and cut. Using a yarn needle, thread the tail through all the stitches on the needle and pull tight. Don't cut the yarn yet; the rest is used for seaming.

SEAM

Fold the sock with wrong sides together. Match up the slipped edge stitches and pin in place.

With the crochet hook, slip stitch knitwise from the front for the Big Toe. Pull the end to the WS.

Next slip stitch the seam knitwise from the front for the Main Toe Section and join the intersection neatly.

Continue the seam from the Main Toe Section up the leg to the cuff.

Weave in ends. Block as desired.

Right Sock

Work as for Left Sock to Short-Row Heel.

SHORT-ROW HEEL

Setup Row (RS) Slip 1, k11 (13) place marker; continue short-row heel on next 32 (36) stitches as for Left Sock.

Work Foot as for Left Sock to Toe Setup.

TOE SETUP

Row 1 (RS) Slip 1, k22 (26), M1, k2, M1, k39 (43) — 66 (74) stitches.

Row 2 Slip 1, purl to end.

Continuing in stockinette stitch and slipping the first stitch of every row, increase by working an e-wrap before the first marker and after the second marker every RS row 3 more times, ending with a WS row; remove markers — 72 (80) stitches with 28 (32) stitches for Big Toe Section and 44 (48) stitches for Main Toe Section.

Division Row (RS) Slip 1, k43 (47), then transfer these stitches to waste yarn or a stitch holder to Main Toe Section; slip 1, knit to end of row.

Complete sock as for Left Sock, but work the Big Toe Section first, then the Main Toe Section.

Work seams as for Left Sock, but slip stitch purlwise from the back.

Lullaby

Need a quick gift for a new baby?

Moms will appreciate these little booties that stay secure with a crocheted tie threaded through eyelets in the cuff. These are a good way to use up small amounts of yarn. Always keep a few pairs ready for new arrivals.

SIZE	Infant 0–3 months
FINISHED MEASUREMENTS	Circumference: 4" Foot length: 3"
YARN	Cascade Yarns Heritage, fingering weight, 75% superwash wool/25% nylon, 60 yds/0.5 oz, 1 skein Citron #5629
NEEDLES	US 0 (2.0 mm) 9" straight needles *or size needed to obtain gauge*
OTHER SUPPLIES	Waste yarn or small stitch holders, two stitch markers, yarn needle, seaming pins, US F/5 (3.75 mm) crochet hook *or size needed to match the slipped edge stitches* (see Closing the Seam, page 15), 1 yd ¼"–½" ribbon (optional), 1 package ribbon rosette embellishments
GAUGE	32 stitches and 48 rows = 4" in stockinette stitch Knit a swatch for accurate sizing.

TIP

The multicolored socks were made exactly as directed, *except* they were knitted with 60 yards of sport-weight yarn on size 2 needles at a gauge of 24 st × 40 rows = 4". This illustrates the importance of gauge — and shows an easy way to get a different size. Use a calculator, swatch, and plan ahead when substituting yarns and needle sizes.

Both Socks

CUFF

Cast on 37 stitches loosely.

Row 1 (RS) Slip 1, *p1, k1; repeat from * to end.

Rows 2–12 Slipping the first stitch of every row, work 11 more rows in established rib.

Eyelet Row (RS) Slip 1, *yo, k2tog; repeat from * to end.

Row 14 (WS) Slip 1, purl to end.

Row 15 Slip 1, k15, k2tog, knit to end — 36 stitches.

Row 16 Slip 1, purl to end.

HEEL FLAP

Row 1 (RS) Slip 1, k8, transfer these 9 stitches to waste yarn or a small stitch holder; [slip 1, k1] 9 times, turn; transfer remaining 9 stitches to waste yarn or another small stitch holder — 18 flap stitches.

Row 2 Slip 1, p17.

Working flap stitches only, repeat [Rows 1 and 2] 9 times — 18 flap rows.

HEEL TURN

Row 1 (RS) Slip 1, k10, ssk, k1, turn, leaving 4 stitches unworked.

Row 2 (WS) Slip 1, p5, p2tog, p1, turn, leaving 4 stitches unworked.

Row 3 Slip 1, knit to 1 stitch before gap formed on previous row, ssk [1 stitch from each side of gap], k1, turn.

Row 4 Slip 1, purl to 1 stitch before gap formed on previous row, p2tog [1 stitch from each side of gap], p1, turn.

Repeat Rows 3 and 4 once more — 10 stitches.

GUSSET

Row 1 (RS) Knit to end of heel; pick up 9 stitches along the side of the flap, place marker; k9 stitches from holder.

Row 2 Slip 1, purl to end of heel; pick up and purl [from the back of the stitch] 9 stitches along the side of the flap, place marker; p9 stitches from holder — 46 stitches.

Row 3 Slip 1, knit to marker, k1, ssk, knit to 3 stitches before next marker, k2tog, k1, knit to end — 44 stitches.

Row 4 Slip 1, purl to end.

Repeat [Rows 3 and 4] 4 times — 36 stitches.

FOOT

Slipping the first stitch of every row, work even in stockinette stitch for 1", (2¼" from back of heel) or about ¾" shorter than desired length.

ROUND TOE

Row 1 (RS) Slip 1, k1, k2tog, *k2, k2tog; repeat from * to end — 27 stitches.

Rows 2–4 Work even.

Row 5 Slip 1, k2tog, *k1, k2tog, repeat from * to end — 18 stitches.

Row 6 Work even.

Row 7 Slip 1, k1, *k2tog; repeat from * to end — 10 stitches.

Row 8 Slip 1, purl across.

Cut yarn, leaving an 18" tail. Using a yarn needle, thread tail through all stitches and pull tight. Don't cut the yarn yet; the rest is used for seaming.

SEAM

Fold the sock with wrong sides together. Match up the slipped edge stitches and pin in place. Using the crochet hook, slip stitch knitwise from the front into each corresponding set of stitches up to the top of the cuff to close the seam. (See page 15).

Fasten off. Weave in ends. Block as desired.

TIES

Using a crochet hook, chain two ties each about 18" long. Weave ends into chain. Thread ties through the eyelets, then tie in bows. Alternatively, you may use ribbon as ties.

Lullaby

42

Wrapped in Hugs

Sometimes a hug is all we need to set the day right, whether it be from someone in our family or a friend. We all need a reminder that we're loved. This sock begins with a knit 2, purl 2 ribbing that is spiced up with a mock cable twist. The little motif running along the side of the leg has a detail that gives the extended 2 × 2 ribbing a squeeze every so often on the way down.

SIZE	Woman S (M, L)
FINISHED MEASUREMENTS	Circumference: 7 (8, 9)" Foot Length: 8½ (9½, 10½)"
YARN	Creatively Dyed Yarn Steele, fingering weight, 100% superwash merino wool, 510 yds/150 g, 1 skein Door OOAK artisan hand-dyed yarn; Cascade Yarns Heritage, fingering weight, 75% superwash merino wool/25% nylon, 437 yds/100 g, 1 skein Tutu #5613
NEEDLES	US 1 (2.25 mm) 9" straight needles *or size needed to obtain gauge*
OTHER SUPPLIES	4 stitch markers, waste yarn or small stitch holders, yarn needle, seaming pins, US F/5 (3.75 mm) crochet hook *or size needed to match the slipped edge stitches* (see Closing the Seam, page 15)
GAUGE	32 stitches and 40 rows = 4" in stockinette stitch Knit a swatch for accurate sizing.

Pattern Notes

- This sock is designed with a round heel and star toe.
- Don't forget to slip the first stitch of every row purlwise. This is vital to achieving a smooth seam.

Special Abbreviation

T2 (Twist 2) Knit 2nd stitch on the needle but do not remove, knit the first stitch and take both off.

Wrapped Stitch Rib (10-stitch panel)

Row 1 (RS) P2, insert right-hand needle between the 6th and 7th stitches on the left-hand needle and pull the loop through, place loop onto left-hand needle next to first stitch, then knit them together, k1, p2, k2, p2. The wrap should be snug but not overly tight.

Rows 2, 4, 6, and 8 (WS) K2, p2, k2, p2, k2.

Rows 3, 5, and 7 (RS) P2, k2, p2, k2, p2.

Repeat Rows 1–8 for pattern.

Left Sock

CUFF

Cast on 64 (72, 80) stitches loosely.

Row 1 (RS) Slip 1, p2, *k2, p2; repeat from * to last stitch, k1.

Row 2 (WS) Slip 1, k2, *p2, k2; repeat from * to last stitch, p1.

Row 3 Slip 1, p2, T2, p2, *k2, p2, T2, p2; repeat from * to last stitch, end k1.

Row 4 Slip 1, k2, *p2, k2; repeat from * to last stitch, p1.

Repeat Rows 1–4 until piece measures 2½" or desired length.

LEG

Setup Row (RS) Slip 1, k52 (60, 68), place marker, work Wrapped Stitch Rib across 10 stitches, place marker, k1.

Working Wrapped Stitch Rib between markers and all other stitches in stockinette stitch, work even until sock measures 6" or desired length, ending with a WS row.

HEEL FLAP

Row 1 (RS) Slip 1, k1, transfer these 2 stitches to waste yarn or a small stitch holder; [slip 1, k1] 16 (18, 20) times, turn; transfer remaining 30 (34, 38) stitches to waste yarn or another small stitch holder — 32 (36, 40) flap stitches.

Row 2 Slip 1, p31 (35, 39).

Working flap stitches only, repeat [Rows 1 and 2] 15 (17, 19) times — 32 (36, 40) flap rows.

HEEL TURN

Row 1 (RS) Slip 1, k18 (20, 22), ssk, k1, turn, leaving 10 (12, 14) stitches unworked.

Row 2 (WS) Slip 1, p7, p2tog, p1, turn, leaving 10 (12, 14) stitches unworked.

Row 3 Slip 1, knit to 1 stitch before gap formed on previous row, ssk [1 stitch from each side of gap], k1, turn.

Row 4 Slip 1, purl to 1 stitch before gap formed on previous row, p2tog [1 stitch from each side of gap], p1, turn.

Repeat Rows 3 and 4 until all heel stitches have been worked, ending with a WS row — 20 (22, 24) heel stitches remain.

GUSSET

Row 1 (RS) Knit to end of heel; pick up and knit 16 (18, 20) stitches along the side of the flap, place gusset marker; work 32 (34, 38) stitches from holder, maintaining established pattern.

Row 2 Slip 1, work in pattern to marker; purl to end of heel; pick up and purl [from the back of the stitch] 16 (18, 20) stitches along the side of the flap, place gusset marker; p2 from holder — 84 (94, 104) stitches.

Row 3 Slip 1, work to first gusset marker, k1, ssk, knit to 3 stitches before next gusset marker, k2tog, k1, work to end — 82 (92, 102) stitches.

Row 4 Slip 1, purl to end.

Repeat [Rows 3 and 4] 10 (11, 12) times — 64 (72, 80) stitches. Remove gusset markers.

FOOT

Slipping the first stitch of every row, work even in established patterns until foot measures 6½ (7½, 8½)" from back of heel, or 2" shorter than desired length, ending with a WS row.

STAR TOE

Setup Row (RS) Slip 1, k13 (15, 17), k2tog, place marker, *k14 (16, 18), k2tog, place marker, repeat from * to end — 60 (68, 76) stitches.

Row 2 (WS) Slip 1, purl to end.

Row 3 (RS Decrease Row) Slipping the first stitch, *knit to 2 stitches before marker, k2tog, slip marker; repeat from * to end — 56 (64, 72) stitches.

Repeat [Rows 2 and 3] 6 (7, 8) times — 32 (36, 40) stitches.

Next Row (WS Decrease Row) Slip 1, ssp, purl to marker, *p2tog, purl to marker; repeat from * to end — 28 (32, 36) stitches.

Repeat RS and WS Decrease Rows until 8 stitches remain, ending with a WS row.

> **Note** For size S and L, the last purl row is worked even without decreases.

Measure the yarn out to about five times the length of sock and cut. Using a yarn needle, thread tail through all stitches and pull up tight. Don't cut the yarn yet; the rest is used for seaming.

SEAM

Fold the sock with wrong sides together. Match up the slipped edge stitches and pin in place. Using the crochet hook, slip stitch knitwise from the front into each corresponding set of stitches up to the top of the cuff to close the seam. (See page 15.)

Fasten off. Weave in ends. Block as desired.

Right Sock

Work Cuff as for Left Sock.

LEG

Setup Row (RS) Slip 1, place marker, work Wrapped Stitch Rib across 10 stitches, place marker, k53 (61, 69).

Complete Leg as for Left Sock.

HEEL FLAP

Row 1 (RS) Slip 1, k29 (33, 37), transfer these 30 (34, 38) stitches to waste yarn or a small stitch holder; [slip 1, k1] 16 (18, 20) times, turn; transfer remaining 2 stitches to waste yarn or another small stitch holder — 32 (36, 40) flap stitches.

Row 2 Slip 1, purl 31 (35, 39), turn.

Complete Heel Flap and Heel Turn as for Left Sock.

GUSSET

Row 1 (RS) Knit to end of heel; pick up and k16 (18, 20) stitches along the side of the flap, place marker; k30 (34, 38) from holder, maintaining Wrapped Rib pattern.

Row 2 Slip 1, purl to end of heel; pick up and purl [from the back of the stitch] 16 (18, 20) stitches along the side of the flap, place marker; work 2 stitches from holder, maintaining established pattern — 84 (94, 104) stitches.

Continue as for Left Sock until Star Toe is complete.

SEAM

Work as for Left Sock, but slip stitch purlwise from the back to close the seam.

Wrapped in Hugs

Blue Tranquility

Take it easy, lay back, and gaze up at the sky on a cloudless day, or toss pebbles into a pool of water; take time to slow down and be calm. This pretty blue sock features a simple stair-step pattern that creates a very elastic, close-fitting sock that finishes with a round-toe variation.

SIZES	Woman S (M)
FINISHED MEASUREMENTS	Circumference: 6 (6½)", unstretched Foot length: 8½ (9)"
YARN	Universal Yarn Pace, fingering weight, 75% superwash wool / 25% nylon, 220 yds / 50 g, 2 skeins Pewter #11
NEEDLES	US 1 (2.25 mm) 9" straight needles *or size needed to obtain gauge*
OTHER SUPPLIES	8 stitch markers, split-ring stitch marker, waste yarn or stitch holder, US F/5 (3.75 mm) crochet hook *or size needed to match the slipped edge stitches* (see Closing the Seam, page 15)
GAUGE	32 stitches and 48 rows = 4" in stockinette stitch 40 stitches and 48 rows = 4" in Broken Diagonal Rib Knit a swatch for accurate sizing.

Broken Diagonal Rib (multiple of 6 stitches + 4)

Rows 1 and 3 (RS) K4, *p2, k4; repeat from * to end.

Rows 2 and 4 (WS) P4, *k2, p4; repeat from * to end.

Rows 5 and 7 K2, *p2, k4; repeat from * to last 2 stitches, p2.

Rows 6 and 8 K2, *p4, k2; repeat from * to last 2 stitches, p2.

Rows 9 and 11 *P2, k4, repeat from * to last 4 stitches, p2, k2.

Rows 10 and 12 P2, k2, *p4, k2, repeat from * to end.

Repeat Rows 1–12 for pattern.

Pattern Notes

- This sock is designed with a round heel and round toe.
- Don't forget to slip the first stitch of every row purlwise throughout. This is vital to achieving a smooth seam.

Left Sock

CUFF

Cast on 65 (71) stitches loosely.

Row 1 (RS) Slip 1, *p1, k1; repeat from * to end.

Slipping the first stitch of every row, work 13 more rows in established rib, decreasing 1 stitch on the last row — 64 (70) stitches.

LEG

Setup Row (RS) Slip 1, p2, place marker; work Broken Diagonal Rib to last 3 stitches, place marker; p2, k1.

Slipping the first stitch of every row, work even in established pattern until piece measures about 6¼", and ending with Row 4 of stitch pattern — 64 (70) stitches.

HEEL FLAP

Row 1 (RS) Slip 1, then transfer this stitch to a split-ring stitch marker to hold; [slip 1, k1] 16 (18) times, turn; transfer remaining 31 (33) stitches to waste yarn or a stitch holder for the instep — 32 (36) flap stitches.

Row 2 Slip 1, p31 (35), turn.

Working flap stitches only, repeat [Rows 1 and 2] 15 (17) times — 32 (36) flap rows worked.

HEEL TURN

Row 1 (RS) Slip 1, k18 (20), ssk, k1, turn, leaving 10 (12) stitches unworked.

Row 2 (WS) Slip 1, p7, p2tog, p1, turn, leaving 10 (12) stitches unworked.

Row 3 Slip 1, knit to 1 stitch before gap formed on previous row, ssk [1 stitch from each side of gap], k1, turn.

Row 4 Slip 1, purl to 1 stitch before gap formed on previous row, p2tog [1 stitch from each side of gap], p1, turn.

Repeat Rows 3 and 4 until all heel stitches have been worked, ending with a WS row — 20 (22) heel stitches remain.

GUSSET

Row 1 (RS) Knit to end of heel; pick up and k16 (18) along the side of the flap; working across 31 (33) stitches from holder, p2, place marker, work established Broken Diagonal Rib across 26 (28) stitches, place marker, p2, k1.

Row 2 Slip 1, k2, work Broken Diagonal Rib to marker, k2, purl to end of heel; pick up and purl (from the back of the stitch) 16 (18) stitches along the side of the flap, p1 from split-ring marker — 84 (92) stitches.

Row 3 Slip 1, k1, ssk, knit to 5 stitches before marker, k2tog, k1, p2, slip marker, work established pattern to next marker, slip marker, p2, k1 — 82 (90) stitches.

Row 4 Slip 1, work in established pattern to end of row.

Repeat [Rows 3 and 4] 9 (9) times — 64 (72) stitches.

FOOT

Slipping the first stitch of every row, work even until foot measures about 6½ (7)" from back of heel, or 2" shorter than desired length, ending with a WS row.

ROUND TOE

Setup Row (RS) Slip 1, k5, k2tog, place marker, *k6, k2tog, place marker, repeat to end — 56 (63) sts.

Continuing in stockinette stitch, work 5 rows even.

Decrease Row (RS) Slip 1, *knit to 2 stitches before marker, k2tog, slip marker, repeat from * to end — 48 (54) stitches.

Repeat Decrease Row every 6th row twice, every 4th row once, then every RS row once, ending with a WS row — 16 (18) stitches.

Next Row Slip 1, k1, k2tog 7 (8) times — 9 (10) stitches.

Blue Tranquility

Last Row Slip 1, p6 (7), ssp — 8 (9) stitches.

Measure the yarn out to about five times the length of sock and cut. Using a yarn needle, thread the tail through all stitches and pull tight. Don't cut the yarn yet; the rest is used for seaming.

SEAM

Fold the sock with wrong sides together. Match up the slipped edge stitches and pin in place. Using the crochet hook, slip stitch knitwise from the front, into each corresponding set of stitches up to the top of the cuff to close the seam. (See page 15.)

Fasten off. Weave in ends. Block as desired.

Right Sock

Work as for Left Sock to Heel Flap.

HEEL FLAP

Row 1 (RS) Slip 1, p2, work 26 (28) stitches in established pattern, p2, then transfer all stitches worked to waste yarn or a stitch holder for the instep; [slip 1, k1] 16 (18) times, turn; transfer last stitch to a split-ring marker to hold — 32 (36) flap stitches.

Row 2 Slip 1, p31 (36).

Complete Heel Flap and Heel Turn as for Left Sock.

GUSSET

Row 1 (RS) Knit across heel; pick up and k16 (18) stitches along the side of the flap, k1 from split-ring marker, turn.

Row 2 Slip 1, purl to end of heel; pick up and purl [from the back of the stitch] 16 (18) stitches along the side of the flap; working across 31 (33) stitches from holder, k2, place marker, work established Broken Diagonal Rib across 26 (28) stitches, place marker, k2, p1.

Row 3 Slip 1, p2, slip marker, work established pattern to marker, slip marker, p2, k1, ssk, knit to last 4 stitches, k2tog, k2 — 82 (90) stitches.

Row 4 Slip 1, work in established pattern to end of row.

Continue as for Left Sock until Round Toe is complete.

SEAM

Work as for Left Sock, but work slip stitch purlwise from the back to close the seam.

Carpentry Squares

The classic squares pattern reminds me of carpentry, the smell of freshly cut wood, and many happy hours spent with my father doing work around the house. He always had a pencil stuck behind his ear and a happy tune to whistle. The textured knit-purl pattern produces a stretchy, ankle-hugging sock.

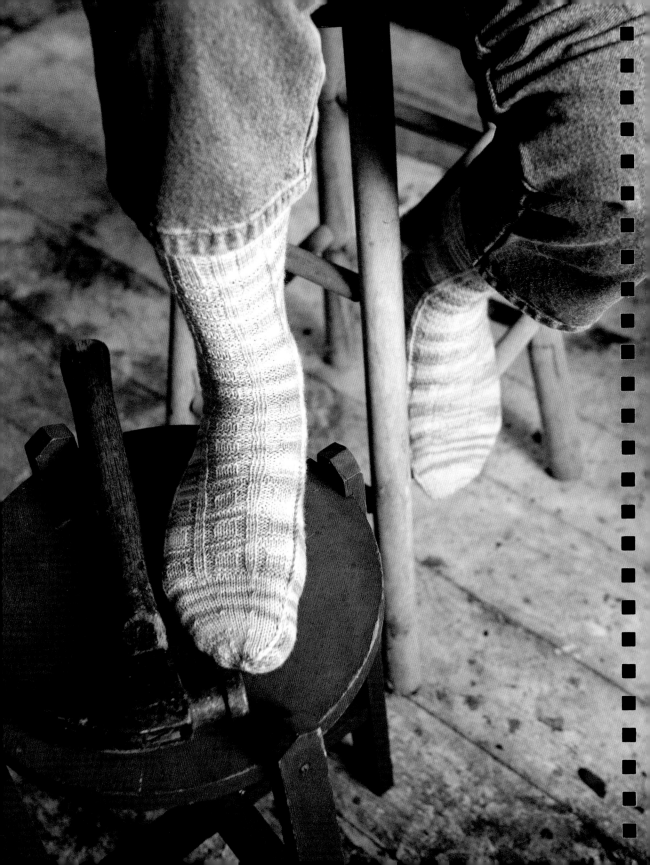

SIZES	Man M (L)
FINISHED MEASUREMENTS	Circumference: 7 (8)" unstretched Foot length: 10 (11)"
YARN	Cascade Heritage Paints, fingering weight, 75% superwash merino wool/ 25% nylon, 437 yds/100 g, 1 skein Wild Honey #9906
NEEDLES	US 1 (2.25 mm) 9" straight needles *or size needed to obtain gauge*
OTHER SUPPLIES	Waste yarn or stitch holders, 2 stitch markers, yarn needle, seaming pins, US F/5 (3.75 mm) crochet hook *or size needed to match the slipped edge* *stitches* (see Closing the Seam, page 15)
GAUGE	32 stitches and 40 rows = 4" in stockinette stitch 40 stitches and 40 rows = 4" in Squares pattern Knit a swatch for accurate sizing.

Squares (multiple of 10 stitches)

Row 1 (RS) Slip 1, knit to end.

Row 2 Slip 1, purl to end.

Rows 3 and 11 Slip 1, *p8, k2; repeat from *, ending last repeat k1.

Rows 4 and 12 Slip 1, *k8, p2; repeat from *, ending last repeat p1.

Rows 5, 7, and 9 Slip 1, *p2, k4, p2, k2; repeat from *, ending last repeat k1.

Rows 6, 8, and 10 Slip 1, *k2, p4, k2, p2; repeat from *, ending last repeat p1.

Repeat Rows 1–12 for pattern.

Pattern Notes

- This sock is designed with a round heel and round toe.
- Don't forget to slip the first stitch of every row purlwise. This is vital to achieving a smooth seam.

Left Sock

CUFF

Cast on 70 (80) stitches loosely.

Row 1 (RS) Slip 1, *p2, k4, p2, k2, repeat from * ending last repeat k1.

Row 2 Slip 1, *k2, p4, k2, p2, repeat from * ending last repeat p1.

Work in established rib until piece measures 2".

LEG

Work the 12-row Squares pattern 5 times.

HEEL FLAP

Row 1 (RS) Slip 1, work 9 stitches in pattern, then transfer 10 stitches just worked to waste yarn or a stitch holder; [slip 1, k1] 15 (20) times, turn; transfer

Carpentry Squares

remaining 30 stitches to waste yarn or another stitch holder — 30 (40) flap stitches.

Row 2 Slip 1, p29 (39).

Working flap stitches only, repeat [Rows 1 and 2] 14 (19) times — 30 (40) flap rows.

HEEL TURN

Row 1 (RS) Slip 1, k18 (22), ssk, k1, turn, leaving 8 (14) stitches unworked.

Row 2 (WS) Slip 1, p9 (7), p2tog, p1, turn, leaving 8 (14) stitches unworked.

Row 3 Slip 1, knit to 1 stitch before gap formed on previous row, ssk [1 stitch from each side of gap], k1, turn.

Row 4 Slip 1, purl to 1 stitch before gap formed on previous row, p2tog [1 stitch from each side of gap], p1, turn.

Repeat Rows 3 and 4 until all heel stitches have been worked, ending with a WS row — 20 (24) heel stitches remain.

GUSSET

Row 1 (RS) Knit to end of heel; pick up and knit 15 (20) stitches along the side of the flap, place marker; work 30 stitches from holder in pattern.

Row 2 Slip 1, work in pattern to marker; purl to end of heel; pick up and purl [from the back of the stitch] 15 (20) stitches along the side of the flap, place marker; work 10 stitches from holder in pattern.

Row 3 Slip 1, work in pattern to marker, k1, ssk, knit to 3 stitches before next marker, k2tog, k1, work in pattern to end — 88 (102) stitches.

Row 4 Slip 1, work in pattern to marker, purl to next marker, work in pattern to end.

Repeat [Rows 3 and 4] 9 (11) times — 70 (80) stitches. Remove markers.

FOOT

Slipping the first stitch of every row, work even in established patterns until foot measures 8 (9)" from back of heel, or about 2" shorter than desired length, increasing 2 (0) stitches evenly across the last row — 72 (80) stitches.

ROUND TOE

Row 1 (RS) Slip 1, k5, k2tog, *k6, k2tog; repeat from * to end — 63 (70) stitches.

Work 5 rows even.

Decrease Row (RS) Slip 1, *knit to 2 stitches before marker, k2tog, repeat from * to end — 54 (60) stitches.

Repeat Decrease Row every 6th row twice, every 4th row once, then every RS row once, ending with a WS row — 18 (20) stitches.

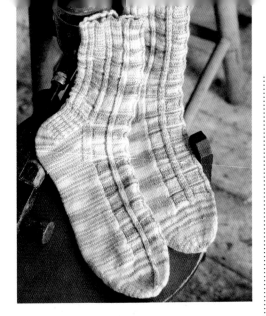

Next Row Slip 1, k1, *k2tog; repeat from * to end — 10 (11) stitches.

Last Row Slip 1, purl to last 2 stitches, ssp — 9 (10) stitches.

Measure the yarn out to about five times the length of the sock and cut. Using a yarn needle, thread the tail through all stitches and pull tight. Don't cut the yarn yet; the rest is used for seaming.

SEAM

Fold the sock with wrong sides together. Match up the slipped edge stitches and pin in place. Using the crochet hook, slip stitch knitwise from the front into each corresponding set of stitches up to top of the cuff to close the seam. (See page 15.)

Fasten off. Weave in ends. Block as desired.

Right Sock

Work as for Left Sock to Heel Flap.

HEEL FLAP

Row 1 (RS) Slip 1, work 29 stitches in pattern, then transfer 30 stitches just worked to waste yarn or a stitch holder; [slip 1, k1] 15 (20) times, turn; transfer remaining 10 stitches to waste yarn or another stitch holder — 30 (40) flap stitches.

Row 2 Slip 1, p29 (39).

Complete Heel Flap and Heel Turn as for Left Sock.

GUSSET

Row 1 Knit to the end of the heel, then pick up and knit 15 (20) stitches along the side of the flap, place marker; work 10 stitches from holder in pattern.

Row 2 Slip 1, work in pattern to marker; purl to end of heel; pick up and purl [from the back of the stitch] 15 (20) stitches along the side of the flap, place marker; work 30 stitches from holder in pattern — 90 (104) stitches.

Continue as for Left Sock until Round Toe is complete.

SEAM

Work as for Left Sock, but work slip stitch purlwise from the back to close the seam.

Carpentry Squares

57

Maple Seed Whirlies

I love to just sit and watch the maple seeds falling and twirling in the sunlight. Kids like to play helicopter with them. The small allover pattern that dots the stockinette stitch background of this sock looks like tiny maple seeds and complements the mirrored stitch pattern that accents the seam running down the side of the socks and onto the toe.

SIZE	Woman M
FINISHED MEASUREMENTS	Circumference: 7" Foot length: 9"
YARN	FatCatKnits hand-dyed sock yarn, fingering weight, 75% superwash wool/25% nylon, 400 yds/100 g, 1 skein OOAK artisan hand-dyed yarn
NEEDLES	US 1 (2.25 mm) 9" straight needles *or size needed to obtain gauge*
OTHER SUPPLIES	Cable needle, waste yarn or small stitch holders, two stitch markers, yarn needle, seaming pins, US F/5 (3.75 mm) crochet hook *or size needed to match the slipped edge stitches* (see Closing the Seam, page 15)
GAUGE	32 stitches and 40 rows = 4" in stockinette stitch Knit a swatch for accurate sizing.

Special Abbreviations

1/2 RC (1 over 2 Right Cross)
Slip 2 stitches to cable needle and
hold in back, k1, k2 from cable needle.

1/3 LC (1 over 3 Left Cross)
Slip 1 stitch to cable needle and hold
in front, k3, k1 from cable needle.

1/3 RC (1 over 3 Right Cross)
Slip 3 stitches to cable needle and
hold in back, k1, k3 from cable needle.

LT (Left Twist) Skip first stitch and
knit next stitch in the back loop, leaving it on needle; knit first and 2nd
stitches together through their back
loops, then slip both stitches onto
right-hand needle together.

RT (Right Twist) K2tog, leaving them
on left-hand needle; knit first stitch
again, then slip both stitches onto
right-hand needle together.

Small Twist (multiple of 8 stitches + 6)

Row 1 (RS) K1, *[LT, RT, k4] 6 times,
LT, RT, k1.
Rows 2–4 Work in stockinette stitch.
Row 5 K5, *[LT, RT, k4] 6 times, k1.
Rows 6–8 Work in stockinette stitch.
Repeat Rows 1–8 for pattern.

Pattern Notes

- This sock is designed with a round heel and a variation of the traditional wedge toe
  with decreases at the sides of the foot; the featured stitch pattern runs down and
  "off" the toe. The pattern also includes the option for a round toe.

- Don't forget to slip the first stitch of every row purlwise. This is vital to achieving a
  smooth seam.

Left Sock

CUFF

Cast on 96 stitches loosely.

Row 1 (RS) Slip 1, k4, [p2, k4] 14 times, p2, k5.

Row 2 Slip 1, p4, [k2, p4] 14 times, k2, p5.

Row 3 Slip 1, 1/3 RC, [p2, ssk, k2tog] 14 times, p2, 1/3 LC, k1 — 68 stitches.

Row 4 Slip 1, p4, [k2, p2] 14 times, k2, p5.

Row 5 Slip 1, k4, [p2, k2] 14 times, p2, k5.

Row 6 Slip 1, p4, [k2, p2] 14 times, k2, p5.

Row 7 Slip 1, 1/3 RC, [p2, k2] 14 times, p2, 1/3 LC, k1.

Repeat Rows 4–7 until piece measures 2", ending with Row 6.

LEG

Row 1 (RS) Slip 1, 1/3 RC, p2, work Row 1 of Small Twist pattern to last 7 stitches, p2, 1/3 LC, k1.

Continuing to work 1/3 RC at beginning of row and 1/3 LC at end of row every 4th row as established and Small Twist pattern over center 54 stitches, work even until piece measures approximately 7", ending with Row 4 of Small Twist pattern.

HEEL FLAP

Row 1 (RS) Slip 1, 1/3 RC, p2, transfer these 7 stitches to waste yarn or a small stitch holder; [slip 1, k1] 17 times, turn; transfer remaining 27 stitches to waste yarn or another small stitch holder — 34 flap stitches.

Row 2 Slip 1, p33.

Working flap stitches only, repeat [Rows 1 and 2] 16 times — 34 flap rows.

HEEL TURN

Row 1 (RS) Slip 1, k18, ssk, k1, turn, leaving 12 stitches unworked.

Row 2 (WS) Slip 1, p5, p2tog, p1, turn, leaving 12 stitches unworked.

Row 3 Slip 1, knit to 1 stitch before gap formed on previous row, ssk [1 stitch from each side of gap], k1, turn.

Row 4 Slip 1, purl to 1 stitch before gap formed on previous row, p2tog [1 stitch from each side of gap], p1, turn.

Repeat Rows 3 and 4 until all heel stitches have been worked, ending with a WS row — 20 heel stitches remain.

GUSSET

Row 1 (RS) Knit to end of heel; pick up and knit 17 stitches along the side of the flap, place marker; work across 27 stitches from holder, maintaining established pattern.

61

Maple Seed Whirlies

Row 2 Slip 1, work established pattern to marker; purl to end of heel; pick up and purl 17 stitches along the side of the flap, place marker; k2, p5 across stitches from holder — 88 stitches.

Row 3 Slip 1, work to marker, k1, ssk, knit to 3 stitches before next marker, k2tog, k1, work in pattern to end — 86 stitches.

Row 4 Slip 1, work in established pattern to end.

Repeat [Rows 3 and 4] 9 times — 68 stitches.

FOOT

Slipping the first stitch of every row and maintaining established patterns, work even until foot measures approximately 7", or 2" shorter than desired length, ending with either Row 2 or 6 of Small Twist pattern.

WEDGE TOE

Row 1 (RS) Slip 1, k3, k2tog, k2, ssk, k28, k2tog, k2, ssk, k17, p2, k5 — 64 stitches.

Rows 2, 4, and 6 Slip 1, p4, k2, purl across.

Row 3 Slip 1, k2, k2tog, k2, ssk, k26, k2tog, k2, ssk, k16, p2, 1/3 LC, k1 — 60 stitches.

Row 5 Slip 1, k1, k2tog, k2, ssk, k24, k2tog, k2, ssk, k15, p2, k5 — 56 stitches.

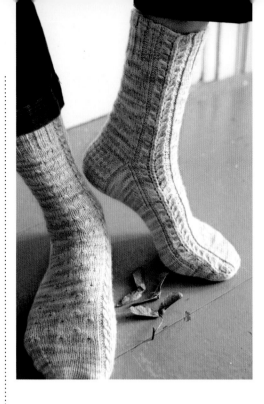

Row 7 Slip 1, k2tog, k2, ssk, k22, k2tog, k2, ssk, k14, p2, 1/3 LC, k1 — 52 stitches.

Row 8 Slip 1, p4, k2, purl to last 2 stitches, ssp — 51 stitches.

Row 9 Slip 1, k2, ssk, k20, k2tog, k2, ssk, k13, p2, k3, k2tog — 47 stitches.

Rows 10 and 12 Slip 1, p3, k2, purl across.

Row 11 Slip 1, k2, ssk, k18, k2tog, k2, ssk, k12, p2, 1/2 LC, k1 — 44 stitches.

Row 13 Slip 1, k2, ssk, k16, k2tog, k2, ssk, k11, p2, k2, k2tog — 40 stitches.

Row 14 Slip 1, p2, k2, purl across.

Row 15 Slip 1, k2, ssk, k14, k2tog, k2, ssk, k10, p2, k1, k2tog — 36 stitches.

Row 16 Slip 1, p1, k2, purl across.

Maple Seed Whirlies

Row 17 Slip 1, k2, ssk, k12, k2tog, k2, ssk, k9, p2, k2tog — 32 stitches.

Row 18 Slip 1, ktog, p8, ssp, p2, p2tog, p10, ssp, p3 — 28 stitches.

Row 19 Slip 1, k2, ssk, k8, k2tog, k2, ssk, k7, k2tog — 24 stitches.

Row 20 Slip 1, ssp, p4, ssp, p2, p2tog, p6, ssp, p3 — 20 stitches.

Row 21 Slip 1, k2, ssk, k4, k2tog, k2, ssk, k3, k2tog — 16 stitches.

Row 22 Slip 1, ssp, ssp, p2, p2tog, p2, ssp, p1, ssp — 11 stitches.

Row 23 Slip 1, k1, ssk, k2tog, k2, ssk, k1 — 8 stitches.

Row 24 Slip 1, purl to end.

Measure the yarn out to about five times the length of the sock and cut. Using yarn needle, thread tail through all stitches and pull up tight. Don't cut the yarn yet; the rest is used for seaming.

OPTIONAL ROUND TOE

Row 1 (RS) Slip 1, knit and decrease 4 stitches evenly across — 64 stitches.

Row 2 Slip 1, purl to end.

Work Round Toe as for Blue Tranquility Socks (page 51).

SEAM

Fold the sock with wrong sides together. Match up the slipped edge stitches and pin in place. Using the crochet hook, slip stitch knitwise from the front into each corresponding set of stitches up to the top of the cuff to close the seam. (See page 15.)

Fasten off. Weave in ends. Block as desired.

Right Sock

Work as for Left Sock to Heel Flap.

HEEL FLAP

Row 1 (RS) Slip 1, 1/3 RC, p2, k20; transfer these 27 stitches to waste yarn or a small stitch holder; [slip 1, k1] 17 times, turn; transfer remaining 7 stitches to waste yarn or another small stitch holder — 34 flap stitches.

Row 2 Slip 1, p33.

Complete Heel Flap and Heel Turn as for Left Sock.

GUSSET

Row 1 (RS) Knit to end of heel; pick up and knit 17 stitches along the side of the flap, place marker; p2, 1/3 LC, k1 across 7 stitches on holder.

Maple Seed Whirlies

Row 2 Slip 1, work established pattern to marker; purl to end of heel; pick up and purl 17 stitches along the side of the flap, place marker; work across 27 stitches on holder, maintaining established pattern — 88 stitches.

Complete Gusset and Foot as for Left Sock, then work optional Round Toe as for Left Sock or Wedge Toe as follows:

WEDGE TOE

Row 1 (RS) Slip 1, k4, p2, k17, k2tog, k2, ssk, k28, k2tog, k2, ssk, k4 — 64 stitches.

Rows 2, 4, 6, and 8 Slip 1, purl to last 7 stitches, k2, p5.

Row 3 Slip 1, 1/3 RC, p2, k16, k2tog, k2, ssk, k26, k2tog, k2, ssk, k3 — 60 stitches.

Row 5 Slip 1, k4, p2, k15, k2tog, k2, ssk, k24, k2tog, ssk, k2 — 56 stitches.

Row 7 Slip 1, 1/3 RC, p2, k14, k2tog, k2, ssk, k22, k2tog, k2, ssk, k1 — 52 stitches.

Row 9 Slip 1, k4, p2, k13, k2tog, k2, ssk, k20, k2tog, k2, k2tog — 48 stitches.

Row 10 Slip 1, purl to last 7 stitches, k2, p3, ssp — 47 stitches.

Row 11 Slip 1, 1/2 RC, p2, k12, k2tog, k2, ssk, k18, k2tog, k3 — 44 stitches.

Rows 12, 14, and 16 Slip 1, work across, knitting the knits and purling the purls.

Row 13 Slip 1, k2tog, k1, p2, k11, k2tog, k2, ssk, k16, k2tog, k3 — 40 stitches.

Row 15 Slip 1, k2tog, p2, k10, k2tog, k2, ssk, k14, k2tog, k3 — 36 stitches.

Row 17 Slip 1, p2tog, p1, k9, k2tog, k2, ssk, k12, k2tog, k3 — 32 stitches.

Row 18 Slip 1, p2, p2tog, p10, ssp, p2, p2tog, p8, k2tog, p1 — 28 stitches.

Row 19 Slip 1, k2tog, k6, k2tog, k2, ssk, k8, k2tog, k3 — 24 stitches.

Row 20 Slip 1, p2, p2tog, p6, ssp, p2, p2tog, p5, ssp — 20 stitches.

Row 21 Slip 1, k2tog, k2, k2tog, k2, ssk, k4, k2tog, k3 — 16 stitches.

Row 22 Slip 1, p2, p2tog, p2, ssp, p2, p2tog, p1, ssp — 12 stitches.

Row 23 Slip 1, k2tog, k2, ssk, k2tog, k1, k2tog — 8 stitches.

Row 24 Slip 1, purl to end.

SEAM

Work as for Left Sock, but work slip stitch purlwise from the back to close the seam.

Moccasocks

These days "roughing it" away from civilization is a good thing. But sometimes a cabin or country house can be a little too rough. These fringed house boots are designed to fit over leggings or skinny jeans and keep out drafts. Loose ankles transition to a snug, close-fitting foot.

SIZES	Woman S (M, L)
FINISHED MEASUREMENTS	Foot circumference: 7 (8, 9)" Calf circumference: 13 (14, 15)" Foot length: 9 (9½, 10)"
YARN	Cascade Yarns Superwash 128, chunky weight, 100% superwash merino wool, 128 yds / 100 g, 2 skeins Daffodil #821 (MC); Cascade Yarns Superwash 220, worsted weight, 100% superwash merino wool, 220 yds / 100 g, 1 skein Mocha #818 (CC)
NEEDLES	US 9 (5.5 mm) 14" straight needles *or size needed to obtain gauge*
OTHER SUPPLIES	Two stitch markers; waste yarn or stitch holders; yarn needle; seaming pins; US I/9 (5.5 mm) crochet hook *or size needed to match the slipped edge stitches* (see Closing the Seam, page 15); four ¼" wooden beads (optional)
GAUGE	16 stitches and 20 rows = 4" in stockinette stitch Knit a swatch for accurate sizing.

65

Moss Stitch (odd number of stitches)

Row 1 (RS) K1, *p1, k1; repeat from * to end.

Row 2 P1, *k1, p1; repeat from * to end.

Row 3 Repeat Row 2.

Row 4 Repeat Row 1.

Repeat Rows 1–4 for pattern.

Pattern Notes

- This sock is designed with a fold-over flap at the top, a round heel, and a star toe. The heel flap is worked in the Eye of Partridge pattern, in which alternating slip stitches on right-side rows make a dense, lattice-like stitch.

- The seam goes down the center front, so left and right socks are worked the same.

- Ankle is designed to be scrunchy and loose, transitioning to a snug foot after the heel.

- Gusset decreases end under the arch in order to create a snug-fitting heel cup that hugs the foot.

- After completing the fringed flap, don't forget to slip the first stitch of every row purlwise to the end of the sock. This is vital to achieving a smooth seam.

Both Socks

CUFF FLAP

Do *not* slip the first stitch of each row.

With A, cast on 55 (59, 63) stitches.

Work 10 rows in Moss Stitch.

Turning Row (RS): Purl across decreasing (p2tog) 3 stitches evenly across — 52 (56, 60) stitches.

CUFF

Slip the first stitch of every row purlwise from this point.

Eyelet Row (WS) Slip 1, yo, *k2tog, yo; repeat from * to last stitch, k1 — 53 (57, 61) stitches.

Setup Rib (RS) Slip 1, *p1, k1; repeat from * to end.

Slipping the first stitch of every row, work 5 rows in established rib.

LEG

Row 1 (RS) Slip 1, knit across row and decrease 1 stitch — 52 (56, 60) stitches.

Slipping the first stitch, work 11 rows even in stockinette stitch.

Decrease Row (RS) Slip 1, k18 (20, 22), k2tog, place marker, k10, place marker, ssk, k19 (21, 23) — 50 (54, 58) stitches.

Continuing in stockinette stitch, repeat Decrease Row every other row 7 times — 36 (40, 44) stitches.

Work even until sock measures 12" from Turning Row, or desired length to top of heel.

HEEL FLAP

Row 1 (RS) Slip 1, k10 (11, 12), transfer these 11 (12, 13) stitches to waste yarn or a stitch holder; *[slip 1, k1] 7 (8, 9) times, turn; transfer remaining 11 (12, 13) stitches to waste yarn or stitch holder — 14 (16, 18) stitches.

> **Note** This is less than half the total number of stitches.

Row 2 Slip 1, p13 (15, 17).

Row 3 Slip 1, [slip 1, k1] 6 (7, 8) times, k1.

Row 4 Repeat Row 2.

Working flap stitches only, repeat from * until 14 (16, 18) flap rows have been worked.

HEEL TURN

Row 1 (RS) Slip 1, k7 (8, 10), ssk, k1, turn, leaving 3 (4, 4) stitches unworked.

Row 2 (WS) Slip 1, p3 (3, 5), p2tog, p1, turn, leaving 3 (4, 4) stitches unworked.

Row 3 Slip 1, knit to 1 stitch before gap formed on previous row, ssk [1 stitch from each side of gap], k1, turn.

Row 4 Slip 1, purl to 1 stitch before gap formed on previous row, p2tog [1 stitch from each side of gap], p1, turn.

Repeat Rows 3 and 4 until all heel stitches have been worked, ending with a WS row — 8 (10, 12) heel stitches remain.

> **Note** For size S, the last 2 rows end with decreases.

GUSSET

Row 1 (RS) Knit to end of heel; pick up and knit 7 (8, 9) stitches along the side of the flap; k11 (12, 13) stitches from holder.

Row 2 Slip 1, purl to end of heel; pick up and purl [from the back of the stitch] 7 (8, 9) stitches along the side of the flap; p11 (12, 13) stitches from holder — 44 (50, 56) stitches.

Row 3 Slip 1, k12 (14, 15), place marker, ssk, k14 (16, 20), k2tog, place marker, k13 (15, 16) — 42 (48, 54) stitches.

Row 4 Slip 1, purl to end.

Repeat [Rows 3 and 4] 7 (8, 9) times decreasing between markers — 28 (32, 36) stitches.

FOOT

Slipping the first stitch of every row, work even in stockinette stitch until foot measures about 7 (7½, 8)" from back of heel, or about 2" shorter than desired length, ending with a WS row.

STAR TOE

Setup Row (RS) Slip 1, k4 (5, 6), k2tog, place marker, *k5 (6, 7), k2tog, place marker, repeat from * to end — 24 (28, 32) stitches.

Row 2 Slip 1, purl to end.

Row 3 (RS Decrease Row) Slipping the first stitch of each row, *knit to 2 stitches before marker, k2tog; repeat from * to end — 20 (24, 28) stitches.

Repeat Rows 2 and 3 twice — 12 (16, 20) stitches.

Next Row (WS Decrease Row) Slip 1, ssp, purl to marker, *p2tog, purl to marker; repeat from * to end — 8 (12, 16) stitches.

Repeat RS and WS Decrease Rows until 8 stitches remain, working a last purl row without any decreases for size M only.

Measure the yarn out to about five times the length of the sock and cut. Using a yarn needle, thread the tail through all stitches and pull up tight. Don't cut the yarn yet; the rest is used for seaming.

SEAM

Fold the sock with wrong sides together. Match up the slipped edge stitches and pin in place. Using the crochet hook, slip stitch knitwise from the front into each corresponding set of stitches up to the top of the cuff to close the seam. (See page 15).

Fasten off. Weave in ends. Block as desired.

69

Moccasocks

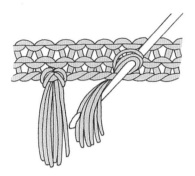

Making the fringe

Overcast stitches on the back-of-the-leg decrease lines

Finished fringe

Overcast stitches on the front seam

FRINGE AND EMBROIDERY

Cut 56 (60, 64) strands of CC 9" long for the fringe; they should be cut longer than the desired finished length. *Hold two pieces together and fold in half. With RS of Flap facing and using the crochet hook, draw the folded end of strands from RS to WS. Pull the loose cut ends through the loop at the fold, and then pull the cut ends to tighten. Repeat from *, spacing every other stitch along the edge. Trim even.

Using yarn needle, a long strand of CC, and overcast stitches, embroider up the front seam and up the decrease lines on the back of the leg. Refer to photo for placement.

CORD

With the crochet hook, chain two cords each about 36" long. Knot the ends and leave ends loose for the moment.

Thread the cord through the eyelets under the cuff. Add a tassel to the ends of the cord or thread a wooden bead onto the yarn tail and secure into cord if desired.

Livin' in Blue Jeans

Classic blue-jeans comfort for your feet will hug every curve just like your favorite pair of denims. DK-weight yarn knits up quickly with contrast "stitching" detail, a picked-up cuff, and a "button-down fly."

SIZES	Woman S (M, L)
FINISHED MEASUREMENTS	Circumference: 7 (7½, 8)" Foot length: 9 (9½, 10)"
YARN	Elsebeth Lavold Silky Wool, DK weight, 45% wool/35% silk/20% nylon, 192 yds/50 g, 2 skeins Neptune Blue #087 (MC) and 1 skein Wheat #099 (CC)
NEEDLES	US 2 (2.75 mm) 9" straight needles *or size needed to obtain gauge* US 1 (2.25 mm) 29" circular needle *or one size smaller than gauge needle*
OTHER SUPPLIES	US G/6 (4 mm) crochet hook *or size needed to match the slipped edge stitches* (see Closing the Seam, page 15), waste yarn or small stitch holders, 6 stitch markers, pins, 2 split-ring stitch markers, thread that matches MC; sewing needle; six ⅝" metal buttons
GAUGE	28 stitches and 36 rows = 4" in stockinette stitch Knit a swatch for accurate sizing.

Pattern Notes

- This sock is designed with a round heel and round toe. The heel is worked in reverse stockinette stitch. The cuff is worked after the rest of the sock is complete.

- Rows of contrast-color yarn are inserted periodically to mimic stitching details on jeans. These rows do not count in row counts.

- The gusset decreases are worked on the sole (under the heel) and end under the arch.

- Don't forget to slip the first stitch of every row purlwise. This is vital to achieving a smooth seam.

Left Sock

LEG

With CC yarn and crochet hook, chain 50 (54, 58) loosely and cut yarn (this is a few more stitches than you need).

With MC and larger needle, pick up and knit 48 (52, 56) stitches through the back bump of the chain.

Row 1 (WS) Slip 1, purl to end.

Slipping the first stitch of every row, work in stockinette stitch for 4" or desired length, ending with a WS row.

HEEL FLAP

Row 1 (RS) Slip 1, k5, then transfer these stitches to waste yarn or a small stitch holder; p24 (26, 28), turn; transfer remaining 18 (20, 22) stitches to waste yarn or another small stitch holder — 24 (26, 28) flap stitches.

Row 2 Slip 1, k23 (25, 27).

Row 3 Slip 1, purl to end of row.

CC Row (WS) Slip 1, join CC and k22 (24, 26), leaving the last stitch unworked; cut CC yarn, then slip all stitches back to the left-hand needle.

Row 4 (WS) Slip 1, with MC, knit to end of row.

Work even in reverse stockinette stitch with MC for 19 (21, 23) more rows, ending with a WS row — do not count the inserted CC row.

HEEL TURN

Row 1 (RS) Slip 1, p12 (14, 16), p2tog, p1, turn, leaving 8 stitches unworked.

Row 2 (WS) Slip 1, p3 (5, 7), p2tog, p1, turn, leaving 8 stitches unworked.

Row 3 Slip 1, knit to 1 stitch before gap formed on previous row, ssk [1 stitch from each side of gap], k1, turn.

Row 4 Slip 1, purl to 1 stitch before gap formed on previous row, p2tog [1 stitch from each side of gap], p1, turn.

Repeat Rows 3 and 4 until all heel stitches have been worked, ending with a WS row — 14 (16, 18) heel stitches remain.

GUSSET

Row 1 (RS) Purl to end of heel; pick up and knit 12 (13, 14) stitches along the side of the flap, placing a marker after the first picked-up stitch; k18 (20, 22) stitches from the holder.

Row 2 Slip 1, p29 (32, 35); k14 (16, 18) heel stitches; pick up and purl tbl 12 (13, 14) stitches along the side of the flap, placing

another marker after the first picked-up stitch; p6 stitches from holder — 62 (68, 74) stitches.

Row 3 Slip 1, knit to marker, ssk, purl to 2 stitches before marker, k2tog, slip marker, knit to end — 60 (66, 72) stitches.

Row 4 Slip 1, knit the knit stitches and purl the purl stitches.

Repeat [Rows 3 and 4] 6 (7, 8) times — 48 (52, 56) stitches.

FOOT

Slipping the first stitch of every row, work even in stockinette stitch until foot measures 7 (7½, 8)" from back of heel, or about 2" shorter than desired length, ending with a WS row.

Change to reverse stockinette stitch and work 3 rows.

CC Row (WS) Slip 1, join CC and k46 (50, 54), leaving last stitch unworked; cut CC then slip all stitches back to left-hand needle.

Next Row (WS) With MC, slip 1, knit to end.

For sizes S and L only:

Work 2 rows even.

For size M only:

Next Row (RS) Slip 1, p10, p2tog, [p11, p2tog] twice, p11, ssp — 48 stitches.

Next Row Slip 1, knit to end.

All Sizes:

ROUND TOE

Setup Row (RS) Slip 1, p3 (3, 4), p2tog, [k4 (4, 5), p2tog, place marker] 6 times, p4 (4, 5), ssp — 40 (40, 48) stitches.

Work 3 rows even.

Decrease Row Slip 1, [purl to 2 stitches before marker, p2tog] 6 times, purl to last 2 stitches, ssp — 32 (32, 40) stitches.

Repeat Decrease Row every 4th row once, then every RS row 1 (1, 2) time(s), ending with a WS row — 16 stitches.

Next Row Slip 1, p1, p2tog 6 times, ssp — 9 stitches.

Last Row Slip 1, k6, ssk — 8 stitches.

Cut MC, leaving a 16" tail.

SEAM

Fold the sock with wrong sides together. Match up the slipped edge stitches up to Foot CC Row and pin together. With MC tail and the crochet hook, slip stitch purlwise from the back to close the seam, ending at CC row on the foot; do not fasten off — put split-ring marker in loop to hold it temporarily. Seam will be finished with CC after the cuff is completed.

CUFF

Beginning at the top of the sock, count 30 rows (15 slipped stitches) down the

right edge (edge toward the front of the sock); place a split-ring marker through the slipped edge stitch at this position.

Loosen and pull out CC yarn from provisional cast on and transfer the 47 (51, 55) live stitches to the straight needle, making sure that the needle points toward the marked right edge; set CC cast-on yarn aside.

Row 1 (RS) With circular needle and MC, pick up and knit 15 stitches from the marker to the top of the sock; working across the cast-on stitches, [yo, k1, yo] into the first stitch for corner, k46 (50, 54) — 64 (68, 72) stitches.

Row 2 (WS) Knit.

Livin' in Blue Jeans

Row 3 P15, [p1, k1] in next stitch, p1 in corner stitch, [k1, p1] in next stitch, purl to the end — 66 (70, 74) stitches.

Row 4 Knit.

Row 5 P16, [p1, k1] in the next stitch, p1 in corner stitch, [k1, p1] in the next stitch, purl to the end — 68 (72, 76) stitches.

CC Row (WS) Using CC set aside from cast on, slip 1, knit to last stitch, slip 1; do not turn. Slide all stitches back to the other end of the needle.

Row 6 (WS) With MC, knit.

Row 7 P17, [p1, k1] in next stitch, p1 in corner stitch, [k1, p1] in next stitch, purl to the end — 70 (74, 78) stitches.

Row 8 Knit.

Row 9 Purl.

Row 10 (Turning Row) Purl.

Row 11 K17, CDD, knit to the end — 68 (72, 76) stitches.

Row 12 Purl.

Row 13 K16, CDD, knit to the end — 66 (70, 74) stitches.

Row 14 Purl.

Cut yarn, leaving a 40" tail.

FINISHING

The best way to finish the cuff is to graft the facing to the inside of the sock with this variation of the Kitchener stitch. (page 141):

Using MC tail and yarn needle, *insert needle through the first stitch as if to purl, leave on needle. Stitch down through the selvage stitch just below the edge stitch with the marker and back up through the next stitch. Insert needle through first stitch on the needle as if to knit, then take the stitch off the knitting needle. Repeat from * to graft the facing to the inside of the sock, but to turn the corner, insert the yarn needle through 3 stitches on circular needle as if to purl, stitch through the corner stitch from sock, then insert yarn needle through the 3 stitches on the circular needle as if to knit and take off.

Alternatively, you may simply work a sewn hem. Cut the yarn long enough to sew with. To join the two layers, fold the hem to the inside of the garment and use a yarn needle to sew through each stitch on the needle, then through the edge of the sock.

FINISHING SEAM

With CC, pull a loop through the MC loop on the toe seam and continue to close the seam up to the cuff flap. Cut and finish all ends neatly.

Turn the sock inside out and with MC sew the rest of the seam closed behind the facing.

Turn right side out; using needle and thread, sew three buttons evenly spaced on the flap.

Right Sock

Work as for Left Sock to Heel Flap.

HEEL FLAP

Row 1 (RS) Slip 1, k17 (19, 21) then transfer these stitches to waste yarn or a stitch holder; p24 (26, 28), turn; transfer remaining 6 stitches to waste yarn or another stitch holder — 24 (26, 28) flap stitches.

Row 2 Slip 1, k23 (25, 27).

Complete Heel Flap and Heel Turn as for Left Sock.

GUSSET

Row 1 (RS) Purl to the end of the heel, then pick up and knit 12 (13, 14) stitches along the side of the flap, placing a marker after the first picked-up stitch; k6 from holder.

Row 2 Slip 1, p17 (18, 19); k14 (16, 18) heel stitches, then pick up and purl (from back) 12 (13, 14) stitches along the

Livin' in Blue Jeans

side of the flap, placing another marker after the first picked-up stitch; p18 (20, 22) stitches from holder.

Continue as for Left Sock until Round Toe is complete.

With MC tail, work partial seam as for Left Sock, but slip stitch purlwise from the back.

CUFF

Beginning at the top of the sock, count 30 rows (15 slipped stitches) down the left edge (edge toward the front of the sock); place a marker through the slipped edge stitch at this position.

Loosen and pull out CC yarn from provisional cast on and transfer 47 (51, 55) live stitches to a straight needle, making sure that the needle points toward the unmarked left edge; set CC cast-on yarn aside.

Row 1 (RS) With circular needle and MC, and working across the cast-on stitches, k46 (50, 54), then [yo, k1, yo] in the last [corner] stitch; pick up and knit 15 stitches along the left edge to the marked edge stitch — 64 (68, 72) stitches.

Row 2 (WS) Knit.

Row 3 P46, [p1, k1] in next stitch, p1 in corner stitch, [k1, p1] in next stitch, purl to end.

Row 4 Knit.

Row 5 P47, [p1, k1] in next stitch, p1 [corner stitch], [k1, p1] in next stitch, purl to end.

CC Row (WS) Using CC set aside from cast on, slip 1, knit to the last stitch, slip 1; do not turn work. Slide all stitches back to the other end of the needle.

Row 6 (WS) With MC, knit.

Row 7 P48, [p1, k1], in next stitch, p1 in corner stitch, [k1, p1] in next stitch, purl to end.

Row 8 Knit.

Row 9 Purl.

Row 10 (Turning Row) Purl.

Row 11 K48, CDD, knit to end.

Row 12 Purl.

Row 13 K47, CDD, knit to end.

Row 14 Purl.

Cut yarn, leaving a 40" tail.

Finish cuff and complete seam as for Left Sock.

Thread a sewing needle and sew on three buttons.

Fireside

Toasting your toes by the fire is a very homey thing to do. But if you can't warm your feet up that way, try these nice, thick, cushy waffle-textured socks that are easy and quick to knit in a DK weight. A little touch of contrast knitting adds interest.

SIZES	Man S (M, L)
FINISHED MEASUREMENTS	Circumference: 7 (7½, 8)", unstretched Foot length: 9 (9½, 10)"
YARN	Berroco Vintage DK, DK weight, 50% acrylic/40% wool/10% nylon, 288 yds/100 g, 2 skeins Cracked Pepper #2107 (MC) and 1 skein Cast Iron #2145 (CC)
NEEDLES	US 2 (2.75 mm) 9" straight needles *or size needed to obtain gauge*
OTHER SUPPLIES	Waste yarn or small stitch holders, two stitch markers, yarn needle, seaming pins, US G/6 (4 mm) crochet hook *or size needed to match the slipped edge stitches* (see Closing the Seam, page 15)
GAUGE	28 stitches and 36 rows = 4" in stockinette stitch 32 stitches and 36 rows = 4" in Waffle Stitch pattern Knit a swatch for accurate sizing.

Waffle Stitch (multiple of 4 stitches)

Row 1 (RS) Slip 1, knit to end.
Row 2 Slip 1, purl to end.
Row 3 Slip 1, *p2, k2; repeat from * to last 3 stitches, p2, k1.
Row 4 Slip 1, *k2, p2; repeat from * to last 3 stitches, k2, p1.
Repeat Rows 1–4 for pattern.

Pattern Notes

- This sock is designed with a round heel and star toe.
- To join CC color for stripe: On RS row slip first stitch purl-wise, bring new color to the front *between* the needles to purl, keeping the tail in the back.
- Don't forget to slip the first stitch of every row purlwise. This is vital to achieving a smooth seam.

Left Sock

CUFF

With MC, cast on 56 (60, 64) stitches loosely.

Row 1 (RS) Slip 1, *p2, k2, repeat from * ending p2, k1.

Row 2–4 Slipping the first stitch of every row, work in established rib. Do not cut MC yarn; when CC rows are done, bring MC loosely up the side and begin using again.

Rows 5 and 6 Slip 1, join C1, work 2 rows in established rib. Do not cut C1 yarn.

Rows 7 and 8 Slip 1, join C2, work 2 rows in established rib. Cut C2.

Rows 9 and 10 Slip 1, with C1, work 2 rows in established rib. Cut C1.

Rows 11–14 With MC, work 4 more rows in established rib.

LEG

Change to Waffle Stitch pattern and MC; work even until piece measures 6–7" or desired length to heel, ending with Row 4. Heel flap will begin on Row 1 of Waffle stitch pattern, which is simply a knit row. The heel flap will be centered between columns of pattern stitches; this will affect the number of stitches used for the heel flap.

HEEL FLAP

Row 1 (RS) Slip 1, k2 (1, 2), transfer these 3 (2, 3) stitches to waste yarn or a small stitch holder; [slip 1, k1] 13 (15, 15) times, turn; transfer remaining 25 (28, 29) stitches to waste yarn or another small stitch holder — 26 (30, 30) flap stitches.

Row 2 Slip 1, p25 (29, 29), turn.

Repeat [Rows 1 and 2] 12 (13, 14) times — 28 (30, 32) flap rows.

Fireside

HEEL TURN

Row 1 (RS) Slip 1, k14 (16, 16), ssk, k1, turn, leaving 9 (10, 10) stitches unworked.

Row 2 (WS) Slip 1, p5 (5, 5), p2tog, p1, turn, leaving 9 (10, 10) stitches unworked.

Row 3 Slip 1, knit to 1 stitch before gap formed on previous row, ssk [1 stitch from each side of gap], k1, turn.

Row 4 Slip 1, purl to 1 stitch before gap formed on previous row, p2tog [1 stitch from each side of gap], p1, turn.

Repeat Rows 3 and 4 until all heel stitches have been worked, ending with a WS row — 16 (20, 20) heel stitches remain.

GUSSET

Row 1 (RS) With MC, knit to end of heel; pick up and knit 14 (15, 16) along the side of the flap, place marker; k25 (28, 29) stitches from holder (Row 1 of stitch pattern).

Row 2 Slip 1, purl to end of heel; pick up and purl tbl 14 (15, 16) stitches along the side of the flap, place marker; p3 (2, 3) stitches from holder (Row 2 of stitch pattern) — 74 (78, 84) stitches.

Row 3 Slip 1, continue established Waffle Stitch pattern to marker, slip marker, k1, ssk, knit to 3 stitches before next marker, k2tog, k1, slip marker, continue established Waffle Stitch pattern to end — 72 (76, 82) stitches.

Row 4 Slip 1, work even in Waffle Stitch pattern before the first marker and after the second marker and in stockinette stitch between markers.

Repeat [Rows 3 and 4] 8 (8, 9) times — 56 (60, 64) stitches. Remove markers.

FOOT

Slipping the first stitch of every row, work even in Waffle stitch until foot measures about 7 (7½, 8)" from back of heel, or about 2" shorter than desired length.

STAR TOE

Setup Row (RS) Slip 1, k11 (12, 13), k2tog, place marker, *k12 (13, 14), k2tog, place marker, repeat from * to end — 52 (56, 60) stitches.

Row 2 Slip 1, purl to end.

Row 3 (RS Decrease Row) Slip 1, *knit to 2 stitches before the marker, k2tog; repeat from * to end — 48 (52, 56) stitches.

Repeat [Rows 2 and 3] 5 (6, 6) times — 28 (28, 32) stitches.

Next Row (WS Decrease Row) Slip 1, ssp, purl to marker, *p2tog, purl to marker; repeat from * to end — 24 (24, 28) stitches.

Repeat RS and WS Decrease Rows until 8 stitches remain, working a last purl row without any decreases for sizes S and M.

Measure the yarn out to about five times the length of sock and cut. Using a yarn needle, thread the tail through all stitches and pull up tight. Don't cut the yarn yet; the rest is used for seaming.

SEAM

Fold the sock with wrong sides together. Match up the slipped edge stitches and pin in place. Using the crochet hook, slip stitch knitwise from the front into each corresponding set of stitches up to the top of the cuff to close the seam. (See page 15.)

Fasten off. Weave in ends. Block as desired.

Right Sock

Work as for Left Sock to Heel Flap.

HEEL FLAP

Row 1 (RS) Slip 1, k24 (27, 28), then transfer these stitches to waste yarn or a small stitch holder. *[Slip 1, k1] 13 (15, 15) times, turn; transfer remaining 3 (2, 3) stitches to waste yarn or another small stitch holder — 26 (30, 30) flap stitches.

Row 2 Slip 1, p25 (29, 29).

Complete the Heel Flap and Heel Turn as for Left Sock.

GUSSET

Row 1 (RS) With MC, knit to end of heel; pick up and knit 14 (15, 16) stitches along the side of the flap, place marker; k3 (2, 3) stitches from holder (Row 1 of stitch pattern).

Row 2 Slip 1, purl to end of heel; pick up and purl [from the back of the stitch] 14 (15, 16) stitches along the side of the flap, place marker; p25 (28, 29) stitches from holder (Row 2 of stitch pattern) — 74 (78, 84) stitches.

Continue as for Left Sock until Star Toe is complete.

SEAM

Work as for Left Sock, but slip stitch purl-wise from the back to close the seam.

Fireside

Cirque du Sole

The big-top circus brings bright lights, music and laughter, popcorn and cotton candy, and acrobats and jugglers. Bring a little of that fun home with these cute, colorful socks with contrast soles that resemble little slippers.

SIZES	Child S (M, L)
FINISHED MEASUREMENTS	Circumference: 4¼ (5½, 6¾)", unstretched Foot length: 5½ (6, 7)"
YARN	Hobby Lobby Baby Bee Sweet Delight Pomp, sport weight, 54% acrylic / 36% poly-amide / 10% rayon, 340 yds / 4 oz, 1 skein each Crayons #2115 (MC) and Grape Jelly #290 (CC)
NEEDLES	Size 2 (2.75 mm) 9" straight needles *or size needed to obtain gauge*
OTHER SUPPLIES	Waste yarn or stitch holders, two stitch markers, yarn needle, seaming pins, US F/5 (3.75 mm) crochet hook *or size needed to match the slipped edge stitches* (see Closing the Seam, page 15)
GAUGE	28 stitches and 36 rows = 4" in stockinette stitch 32 stitches and 36 rows = 4" in Garter Rib, unstretched Knit a swatch for accurate sizing.

Garter Rib (multiple of 5 stitches + 4)

Row 1 (RS) Slip 1, p2, *k1, p1, k1, p2; repeat from * to last stitch, k1.

Row 2 Slip 1, p3, *k1, p4; repeat from * to end.

Repeat Rows 1 and 2 for pattern.

Pattern Notes

- This sock is designed with a round heel and star toe.
- The seam goes down the center front, so left and right socks are worked the same.
- Don't forget to slip the first stitch of every row purlwise. This is vital to achieving a smooth seam.

Both Socks

RUFFLED CUFF

With CC, cast on 68 (88, 108) stitches.

Rows 1–5 Slipping the first stitch of every row and beginning with a WS (purl) row, work in stockinette stitch, ending last row with ssp — 67 (87, 107) stitches.

Row 6 (RS) Slip 1, *k2tog; repeat from * to end — 34 (44, 54) stitches.

Row 7 Slip 1, purl to end. Cut CC.

LEG

Row 1 (RS) Change to MC, slip 1, p2, *k1, p1, k1, repeat from * to end.

Row 2 (WS) Slip 1, p3, *k1, p4, repeat from * to end.

Work even in established pattern until piece measures 3½ (4, 4½)" or desired length to top of heel, ending with a WS row.

HEEL FLAP

Row 1 (RS) Slip 1, work 8 (11, 14) stitches in pattern, then transfer these stitches to waste yarn or a stitch holder; join CC, [slip 1, k1] 8 (11, 13) times, turn; transfer remaining 9 (12, 15) stitches to waste yarn or another stitch holder — 16 (22, 26) flap stitches.

Row 2 Slip 1, p15 (21, 25).

Working flap stitches only, repeat [Rows 1 and 2] 7 (10, 12) times — 16 (22, 26) flap rows.

HEEL TURN

Row 1 (RS) Slip 1, k8 (12, 14) ssk, k1, turn, leaving 4 (6, 8) stitches unworked.

Row 2 (WS) Slip 1, p3 (5, 5), p2tog, p1, turn, leaving 4 (6, 8) stitches unworked.

Row 3 Slip 1, knit to 1 stitch before the gap formed on previous row, ssk [1 stitch from each side of gap], k1, turn.

Row 4 Slip 1, purl to 1 stitch before gap formed on previous row, p2tog [1 stitch from each side of gap], p1, turn.

Repeat Rows 3 and 4 until all heel stitches have been worked, ending with a WS row — 10 (14, 16) heel stitches remain.

GUSSET

Row 1 (RS) Knit to the end of the heel; pick up and knit 8 (11, 13) stitches along the side of the flap; join second ball of MC and work 9 (12, 15) stitches from holder in established pattern, placing marker after first stitch.

87

Cirque du Sole

Row 2 (WS) With MC, slip 1, work 8 (11, 14) in stitch pattern; with CC, purl to end of heel, then pick up and purl 8 (11, 13) stitches [from the back of the stitch] along the side of the flap; with MC, work 9 (12, 15) stitches in established pattern, placing marker after first stitch — 44 (58, 70) stitches.

Row 3 With MC, slip 1, work in pattern to marker, ssk; with CC, knit to 2 stitches before next marker, k2tog; with MC, work in pattern to end.

Row 4 Slip 1, work in established patterns and color sequence to end.

Repeat [Rows 3 and 4] 6 (7, 9) times — 32 (44, 52) stitches.

FOOT

Slipping the first stitch of every row, work even, maintaining established patterns and color sequence until foot measures about 3¾ (4¼, 4¾)" from the back of the heel, or about 1¾" shorter than desired length, ending with a RS row.

Next Row (WS) With MC, purl to color change, purl remainder of row with CC, cut MC from both sides.

Work even 2 rows with CC.

STAR TOE

Setup Row (RS) Continuing with CC, slip 1, k5 (8, 10), k2tog, place marker, *k6 (9, 11), k2tog, place marker; repeat from * to end — 28 (40, 48) stitches.

Row 2 Slip 1, purl to end.

Row 3 (RS Decrease Row) Slipping the first stitch, *knit to 2 stitches before marker, k2tog, slip marker; repeat from * to end — 24 (36, 44) stitches.

Repeat [Rows 2 and 3] 2 (3, 4) times — 16 (24, 28) stitches.

Next Row (WS Decrease Row) Slip 1, ssp, purl to marker, *p2tog, purl to marker; repeat from * to end — 12 (20, 24) stitches.

Repeat RS and WS Decrease Rows until 8 stitches remain, working a last purl row without any decreases for sizes S and M.

Cut B, leaving a 12" tail. Using a yarn needle, thread the tail through all stitches and pull up tight. Don't cut the yarn yet; the rest is used for seaming.

SEAM

Fold the sock with wrong sides together. Match up the slipped edge stitches and pin in place. Using the crochet hook, slip stitch into each corresponding set of stitches to close the seam up to 1 stitch before MC edge stitches; pull MC tail through to RS with MC tail, finish closing the seam to the top. (See page 15.)

Fasten off. Weave in ends. Block as desired.

Vroom-Vroom

Here's a basic intarsia sock for the little boys (or girls) who love playing with cars. Watch out — little ones may think they can run faster in these racetrack-inspired socks!

SIZES	Child S (M, L)
FINISHED MEASUREMENTS	Circumference: 6½ (7¼, 8)" Foot length: 7½ (8, 8½)"
YARN	Cascade Yarns Superwash Sport, sport weight, 100% superwash merino wool, 136 yds / 50 g, 1 skein each Really Red #809 (MC), Black #815 (CC1), and White #871 (CC2)
NEEDLES	US 4 (3.5 mm) 9" straight needles *or size needed to obtain gauge*
OTHER SUPPLIES	Three bobbins for yarn colors (optional), waste yarn or small stitch holders, two stitch markers, yarn needle, seaming pins, US G/6 (4 mm) crochet hook *or size needed to match the slipped edge stitches* (see Closing the Seam, page 15)
GAUGE	24 stitches and 32 rows = 4" in stockinette stitch Knit a swatch for accurate sizing.

Pattern Notes

- This sock is designed with a round heel and star toe.
- The colorwork for the Leg is worked using a combination of stranded knitting and intarsia. When working the Leg, use a ball of MC for the wide red section and a smaller ball or bobbin of MC for the 2-stitch side section, and a ball of CC1 and separate 1-yard strands of CC2 for Chart 1. If desired, the Leg may also be worked with MC and CC1 only with (CC2) stripes added in duplicate stitch after the sock is finished.
- The heel flap is worked using stranded knitting; maintain a loose tension when carrying yarn not in use.
- Don't forget to slip the first stitch of every row purlwise. This is vital to achieving a smooth seam.

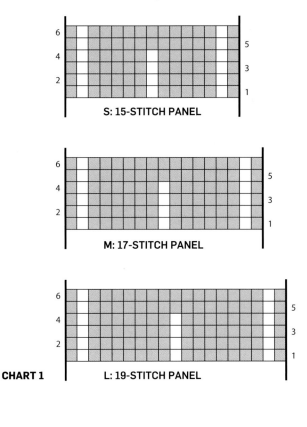

KEY

- MC
- CC1
- CC2
- V Slip 1 at beginning of row

S: 15-STITCH PANEL

M: 17-STITCH PANEL

CHART 1   **L: 19-STITCH PANEL**

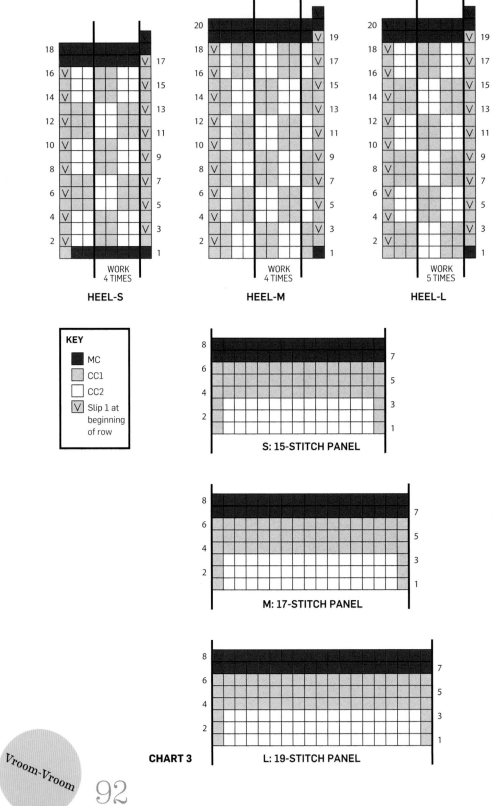

HEEL-S

WORK 4 TIMES

HEEL-M

WORK 4 TIMES

HEEL-L

WORK 5 TIMES

KEY

- ■ MC
- ▨ CC1
- ☐ CC2
- Ⅴ Slip 1 at beginning of row

S: 15-STITCH PANEL

M: 17-STITCH PANEL

CHART 3

L: 19-STITCH PANEL

Left Sock

CUFF

With MC, cast on 40 (44, 48) stitches loosely.

Row 1 (RS) Slip 1, *p2, k2; repeat from * to last 3 stitches, p2, k1.

Slipping the first stitch of every row, work 11 more rows in established rib.

LEG

Color Setup Row (RS) With MC, slip 1, k22 (24, 26); work Row 1 of Chart 1 for your size across the next 15 (17, 19) stitches; k2 to finish row with bobbin of MC.

Continuing in stockinette stitch and slipping the first stitch of every row, work the established color pattern and repeat the 6-row Chart 1 until the piece measures 5" or desired length to the top of the heel.

HEEL FLAP

Row 1 (RS) Slip 1, k1, transfer these 2 stitches to waste yarn or a small stitch holder, cut MC from right side of work only. Do not cut CC1, CC2, or bobbin of MC yarn from work held in reserve — you will need it to resume the pattern after the heel is finished. Joining new balls of CC1 and CC2, work Row 1 of Chart 2 for your size across the next 20 (22, 24) stitches, turn; transfer remaining 18 (20, 22) stitches to waste yarn or another small stitch holder — 20 (22, 24) flap stitches.

Slip the first stitch of every row, follow Chart 2 for the heel flap, changing colors loosely and slipping the first stitch of every row until 18 (20, 20) chart rows are complete; rejoin and finish last rows of chart with MC. Cut CC1 and CC2 from heel flap.

HEEL TURN

Row 1 (RS) Continuing with MC, slip 1, k10 (11, 12), ssk, k1, turn, leaving 6 (7, 8) stitches unworked.

Row 2 (WS) Slip 1, p3, p2tog, p1, turn, leaving 6 (7, 8) stitches unworked.

Row 3 Slip 1, knit to 1 stitch before gap formed on previous row, ssk [1 stitch from each side of gap], k1, turn.

Row 4 Slip 1, purl to 1 stitch before gap formed on previous row, p2tog [1 stitch from each side of gap], p1, turn.

Repeat Rows 3 and 4 until all heel stitches have been worked, ending with a WS row — 12 (13, 14) heel stitches remain.

Note The last two decrease rows for size M do not have a k1 or p1 at the end before the turn.

Vroom-Vroom

GUSSET

Row 1 (RS) With A, knit to the end of the heel, then pick up and knit 9 (10, 10) along the side of the flap, place marker; k18 (20, 22) stitches from holder, maintaining established Chart 1 color pattern.

Row 2 Maintaining color pattern, slip 1, purl to the end of the heel, then pick up and purl 10 (11, 12) stitches along the side of the flap, place marker; p2 from holder — 50 (55, 58) stitches.

Row 3 Maintaining the color pattern, slip 1, knit to marker, ssk, knit to 2 stitches before next marker, k2tog, knit to end — 48 (53, 56) stitches.

Row 4 Maintaining the color pattern, slip 1, purl to end.

Repeat [Rows 3 and 4] 4 (5, 4) times — 40 (44, 48) stitches.

FOOT

Slipping the first stitch of every row and maintaining the established color pattern, work even until the foot measures 5¾ (6, 6½)" from the back of the heel.

Work Chart 3 across the center 15 (17, 19) stitches [formerly Chart 1] finishing chart with MC. Cut CC1 and CC2.

STAR TOE

Setup Row (RS) Continuing only with MC, slip 1, k7 (8, 10), k2tog, place marker, *k8 (9, 10), k2tog, place marker, repeat from * to end — 36 (40, 44) stitches.

Row 2 Slip 1, purl to end.

Row 3 (RS Decrease Row): Slipping the first stitch, *knit to 2 stitches before marker, k2tog; repeat from * to end — 32 (36, 40) stitches.

Repeat [Rows 2 and 3] 2 (3, 4) times — 24 stitches.

Next Row (WS Decrease Row) Slip 1, ssp, purl to marker, *p2tog, purl to marker; repeat from * to end — 20 stitches.

Repeat RS and WS Decrease Rows until 8 stitches remain, ending with a purl row without any decreases.

Measure the yarn out to about five times the length of the sock and cut. Using a yarn needle, thread the tail through all stitches and pull up tight. Don't cut the yarn yet; the rest is used for seaming.

SEAM

Fold the sock with wrong sides together. Match up the slipped edge stitches and pin in place. Using the crochet hook and MC, slip stitch knitwise from the front into each corresponding set of stitches up to the top of the cuff to close the seam. (See page 15.)

Vroom-Vroom

Fasten off. Weave in ends. Block as desired.

Right Sock

Work Cuff as for Left Sock.

LEG

Color Setup Row (RS) With bobbin of MC, slip 1, k1; work Chart 1 for your size across next 15 (17, 19) stitches; k23 (25, 27) with MC from ball.

Continue as for Left Sock to Heel Flap.

HEEL FLAP

Row 1 (RS) Slip 1, k17 (19, 21), transfer these stitches to waste yarn or a small stitch holder. Do not cut CC1, CC2, or bobbin of MC yarn from work held in reserve — you will need it to resume the pattern after the heel is finished. Joining new balls of CC1 and CC2, work Row 1 of Chart 2 for your size across next 20 (22, 24) stitches, turn; transfer remaining 2 stitches of MC to waste yarn or another small stitch holder and cut — 20 (22, 24) flap stitches.

Complete Heel Flap and Heel Turn as for Left Sock.

GUSSET

Row 1 (RS) With MC, knit to end of heel, then pick up and knit 9 (10, 10) stitches

along the side of the flap, place marker; k2 from holder.

Row 2 Slip 1, purl to end of heel, then pick up and purl 10 (10, 10) stitches along the side of the flap, place marker; p18 (20, 22) from holder, maintaining the established Chart 1 color pattern — 52 (57, 62) stitches.

Continue as for Left Sock until Star Toe is complete.

SEAM

Work as for Left Sock, but slip stitch purl-wise from the back to close the seam.

95
Vroom-Vroom

Sláinte

There's a story in my mother's family that our great-great granny was born to a lady-in-waiting in a castle somewhere in County Cork. This sock is in honor of that legend. It features enough cables to make any Celtic lass rejoice. It starts with a sideways cabled cuff adorned with pearl buttons, and then the fun begins. Cheers!

SIZE	Woman M
FINISHED MEASUREMENTS	Circumference: 7", unstretched Foot length: 9"
YARN	Patons Kroy Sock, fingering weight, 75% wool/25% nylon, 166 yds/50 g, 3 skeins Muslin #008
NEEDLES	US 2 (2.75 mm) 9" straight needles *or size needed to obtain gauge*
OTHER SUPPLIES	Cable needle, waste yarn or stitch holders, 7 stitch markers, yarn needle, seaming pins, US G/6 (4 mm) crochet hook *or size needed to match the slipped edge stitches* (see Closing the Seam, page 15), four 11 mm shank pearl buttons, sewing needle, thread to match the yarn
GAUGE	32 stitches and 40 rows = 4" in stockinette stitch Knit a swatch for accurate sizing.

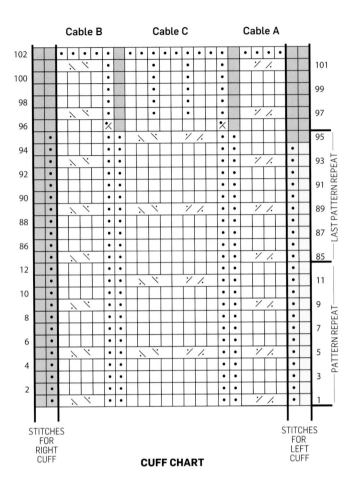

Cable B   **Cable C**   **Cable A**

102 ·
101

100
99

98
97

96
95

94
93

92
91

90
89

88
87

86
85

12
11

10
9

8
7

6
5

4
3

2
1

LAST PATTERN REPEAT

PATTERN REPEAT

STITCHES
FOR
RIGHT
CUFF

STITCHES
FOR
LEFT
CUFF

CUFF CHART

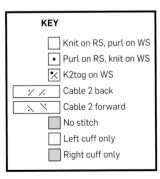

KEY	
	Knit on RS, purl on WS
·	Purl on RS, knit on WS
⊠	K2tog on WS
╱ ╱	Cable 2 back
╲ ╲	Cable 2 forward
	No stitch
	Left cuff only
	Right cuff only

Sláinte

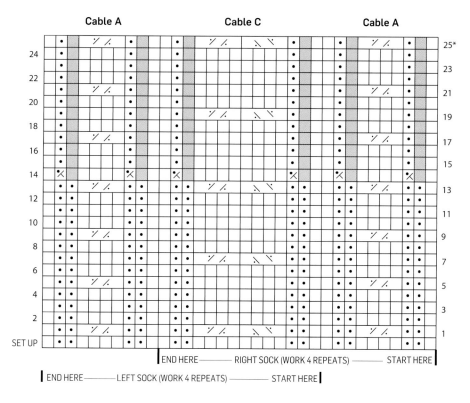

LEG CHART

* Continue in established pattern through 9th repeat of Cable C (Row 49).

Sláinte

Special Abbreviations

2/2 LC (2 over 2 Left Cross) Slip 2 to cable needle and hold in front, k2, k2 from cable needle.

2/2 RC (2 over 2 Right Cross) Slip 2 to cable needle and hold in back, k2, k2 from cable needle.

Cable A (4 stitches)

Row 1 (RS) 2/2 RC.

Row 2 P4.

Row 3 K4.

Row 4 P4.

Repeat Rows 1—4 for pattern.

Cable B (4 stitches)

Row 1 (RS) 2/2 LC.

Row 2 P4.

Row 3 K4.

Row 4 P4.

Repeat Rows 1–4 for pattern.

Cable C (8 stitches)

Rows 1 and 3 (RS) K8.

Rows 2 and 4 P8.

Row 5 2/2 RC, 2/2 LC.

Row 6 P8.

Repeat Rows 1–6 for pattern.

Pattern Notes

- This sock is designed with a round heel and round toe. The cabled cuff is worked sideways with a mini button band; do *not* slip the first stitch of any cuff rows. Leg stitches are picked up from along the side of the cuff and worked down.

- After working the cuff, don't forget to slip the first stitch of every row purlwise. This is vital to achieving a smooth seam.

Sláinte

Left Sock

CUFF

> **Note** Refer to Cuff Chart on page 98.

Cast on 22 stitches.

Setup Row (RS) K1, p1, work Cable A over 4 stitches, p2, work Cable C over 8 stitches, p2, work Cable B over 4 stitches.

Work a total of 94 rows in the established pattern.

Row 95 (RS) Bind off 2 stitches, k4, p2, work Cable C, p2, k4 — 20 stitches.

Row 96 (WS) P4, k2tog, p8, k2tog, p4 — 18 stitches.

Row 97 (RS) Work Work Cable A, [p1, k2] 3 times, p1, work Cable B. There is now a small section of ribbing between Cable A and Cable B.

Rows 98–102 Work these 5 rows in the established pattern, binding off knitwise on the last (WS) row.

LEG

> **Note** Refer to Leg Chart on page 99.

Turn cuff sideways with p1, k1 edge at top; with RS facing, pick up and k96 stitches (1 stitch in every row) along the edge.

Setup Row (WS) Slip 1, [k2, p4, k2, p2, k2, p8, k2, p2] 4 times, ending last repeat with p1 instead of p2.

Row 1 (RS) Beginning with Row 1 of each cable, slip 1, [p2, Cable C, p2, k2, p2, Cable A, p2, k2] 3 times, p2, Cable C, p2, k2, p2, Cable A, p2, k1.

Rows 2–13 Slipping the first stitch of every row, work 12 rows even in the established pattern.

Decrease Row 14 (WS) Slip 1, [k2tog, p4, k2tog, p2, k2tog, p8, k2tog, p2] 3 times, k2tog, p4, k2tog, p2, k2tog, p8, k2tog, p1 — 80 stitches.

Rows 15–49 Slipping the first stitch of every row, work 34 rows even in the established pattern.

Decrease Row 50 (WS) Work 34 stitches in the established pattern, ending at center of Cable C; [p3, p2tog, p1, p2tog, p3, p2tog, p1, p2tog, p4] twice; p4, k1, p1 — 72 stitches.

HEEL FLAP

Row 1 (RS) Work 6 stitches in pattern and transfer to waste yarn or a stitch holder; [slip 1, k1] 16 times, turn; transfer remaining 34 stitches to waste yarn or another stitch holder — 32 flap stitches.

Row 2 Slip 1, p31.Working flap stitches only, repeat [Rows 1 and 2] 15 times — 32 flap rows.

Sláinte

HEEL TURN

Row 1 (RS) Slip 1, k18, ssk, k1, turn, leaving 10 stitches unworked.

Row 2 (WS) Slip 1, p7, p2tog, p1, turn, leaving 10 stitches unworked.

Row 3 Slip 1, knit to 1 stitch before gap formed on previous row, ssk [1 stitch from each side of gap], k1, turn.

Row 4 Slip 1, purl to 1 stitch before gap formed on previous row, p2tog [1 stitch from each side of gap], p1, turn.

Repeat Rows 3 and 4 until all heel stitches have been worked, ending with a WS row — 20 heel stitches remain.

GUSSET

> **Note** Instep stitches begin and end with 4 stitches — half — of Cable C. Continue to turn cables on those 4 stitches as established.

Row 1 (RS) Knit to the end of the heel; pick up and knit 16 stitches along the side of the flap, place marker; work 34 stitches from holder in established pattern.

Row 2 Slip 1, work in pattern to marker; purl to end of heel; pick up and purl [from the back of the stitch] 16 stitches along the side of the flap, place marker; work 6 stitches from holder in established pattern — 92 stitches.

Row 3 Slip 1, work in pattern to first marker, p1, k2tog, knit to 3 stitches before next marker, ssk, p1, work in pattern to end — 90 stitches.

Row 4 Slip 1, work in pattern to marker, k1, purl to 1 stitch before next marker, k1, work in pattern to end.

Repeat [Rows 3 and 4] 9 times — 72 stitches.

FOOT

Slipping the first stitch of every row, work even until the foot measures about 7" from the back of the heel, or about 2" shorter than desired length, ending with a RS row.

Decrease Row (WS) Slip 1, p2tog, p3, p2tog, p1, p2tog, p7, [p2tog, p1, p2tog, p3], remove marker, p32, remove marker, p3, p2tog, p1 — 64 stitches.

ROUND TOE

Setup Row (RS) Slip 1, k5, k2tog, place marker, *k6, k2tog, place marker, repeat from * to end — 56 stitches.

Continuing in stockinette stitch, work 5 rows even.

Decrease Row (RS) Slip 1, *knit to 2 stitches before marker, k2tog, slip marker, repeat from * to end — 48 stitches.

Sláinte

Repeat Decrease Row every 6th row twice, every 4th row once, then every RS row once, ending with a WS row — 16 stitches.

Next Row Slip 1, k1, k2tog 7 times — 9 stitches.

Last Row Slip 1, p6, ssp — 8 stitches.

Measure the yarn out to about five times the length of sock and cut. Using a yarn needle, thread the tail through all stitches and pull tight. Don't cut the yarn yet; the rest is used for seaming.

SEAM

Fold the sock with wrong sides together. Match up the slipped edge stitches and pin in place. Using the crochet hook and the tail from toe, slip stitch knitwise from the front into each corresponding set of stitches up to but not including the cuff to close the seam. (See page 15.)

Fasten off. Weave in ends. Block as desired.

FINISHING

Sew two pearl buttons to the cuff edge with a sewing needle and thread where the 2-stitch bound-off section overlaps the rest of the cuff, going through both layers.

Right Sock

CUFF

Cast on 22 stitches.

Setup Row (RS) Work Cable A over 4 stitches, p2, work Cable C over 8 stitches, p2, work Cable B over 4 stitches, p1, k1.

Work a total of 95 rows in established pattern.

Row 96 (WS) Bind off 2 stitches, k4, k2tog, p8, k2tog, k4 — 18 stitches.

Row 97 Work Cable A, [p1, k2] 3 times, p1, work Cable B. There is now a small section of ribbing between Cable A and Cable B.

Rows 98–102 Work 5 rows in established pattern, binding off knitwise on last WS row.

Sláinte

LEG

Turn cuff sideways with p1, k1 edge at top; with RS facing, pick up and k96 stitches (1 stitch in every row) along the edge.

Setup Row (WS) Slip 1, [k2, p8, k2, p2, k2, p4, k2, p2] 4 times, ending last repeat with p1 instead of p2.

Row 1 (RS) Beginning with Row 1 of each cable, slip 1, [p2, Cable A, p2, k2, p2, Cable C, p2, k2] 3 times, p2, Cable A, p2, k2, p2, Cable A, p2, k1.

Rows 2–13 Slipping the first stitch of every row, work 14 rows even in the established pattern.

Decrease Row 14 (WS) Slip 1, [k2tog, p8, k2tog, p2, k2tog, p4, k2tog, p2] 3 times, k2tog, p8, k2tog, p2, k2tog, p4, k2tog, p1 — 80 stitches.

Rows 15–49 Slipping the first stitch of every row, work 34 rows even in established pattern.

Decrease Row 50 (WS) Slip 1, k1, p4, ending at center of Cable C; [p3, p2tog, p1, p2tog, p3, p2tog, p1, p2tog, p4] twice; work 34 stitches in established pattern — 72 stitches.

HEEL FLAP

Row 1 (RS) Work 34 stitches in pattern and transfer to waste yarn or a stitch holder; [slip 1, k1] 16 times, turn; transfer remaining 6 stitches to waste yarn or another stitch holder — 32 flap stitches.

Row 2 Slip 1, p31.

Complete Flap and Heel Turn as for Left Sock.

GUSSET

Row 1 (RS) Knit to end of heel, then pick up and knit 16 stitches along the side of the flap, place marker; work 6 stitches from the holder in established pattern.

Row 2 Slip 1, work in pattern to marker; purl to end of heel, then pick up and purl [from the back of the stitch] 16 stitches along the side of the flap, place marker; work 34 stitches from the holder in established pattern.

Continue Gusset and Foot as for Left Sock to Decrease Row.

Decrease Row (WS) Slip 1, p2tog, p3, remove marker, p32, remove marker, [p3, p2tog, p1, p2tog] twice, p7, p2tog, p1, p2tog, p3, p2tog, p1 — 64 stitches.

Work Round Toe as for Left Sock.

SEAM

Work as for Left Sock, but slip stitch purlwise from the back to close the seam.

Sláinte

Coffee Break

Coffee breaks have gotten a bit more complicated as we try to decide if we want a cappuccino, espresso, or latte. The choices multiply even more when you think about flavors! If you love coffee, these socks will quench your thirst for style.

SIZE	Woman M
FINISHED MEASUREMENTS	Circumference: 7" Foot length: 9½"
YARN	Cascade Heritage, fingering weight, 75% superwash merino wool/25% nylon, 437 yds/100 g, 1 skein Walnut #5638 (MC) and about 100 yds each Sunflower #5643 (A), Butter #5611 (B), and Snow #5618 (C)
NEEDLES	US 0 (2.0 mm) 9" straight needles *or size needed to obtain gauge*
OTHER SUPPLIES	Four bobbins for yarn colors (optional), waste yarn or small stitch holders, two stitch markers, yarn needle, seaming pins, US F/5 (3.75 mm) crochet hook *or size needed to match the slipped edge stitches* (see Closing the Seam, page 15)
GAUGE	36 stitches and 44 rows = 4" in stockinette stitch 40 stitches and 44 rows = 4" in Lace pattern Knit a swatch for accurate sizing.

Left Sock

CUFF

With MC, cast on 80 stitches loosely. Cut yarn.

Row 1 (RS) Slip 1, join C; knit across.

Row 2 Slip 1, knit to last stitch, p1; cut C.

Row 3 Slip 1, join B; *inc 1 using e-wrap method, k2, ssk, k2tog, k2, inc 1, k2*, repeat from *, ending last repeat with k1.

Row 4 Slip 1, knit to last stitch, p1; cut B.

Row 5 Slip 1, join A, and work as for Row 3.

Row 6 Slip 1, knit to last stitch, p1; cut A.

Rows 7 and 9 Slip 1, join MC, and work as for Row 3.

Rows 8 and 10 With MC, repeat Row 2 but do not cut MC.

LEG

Setup Row (RS) Slipping the first stitch, work the 10-stitch Lace pattern 8 times across the row in the following color sequence: 5 repeats with MC, 1 repeat each with C, B, and A.

Slipping the first stitch of every row, work 13 rows in the established Lace pattern and color sequence.

Coffee Break

Decrease Row (RS) Slip 1, yo, ssk twice, k2tog twice, yo, k1, [k1, yo, ssk twice, k2tog twice, yo, k1] 4 times; work to end of row in established Lace pattern and color sequence — 70 stitches.

Working all MC stitches in stockinette stitch and other colors in established Lace pattern, work even until sock measures 5" or desired length.

HEEL FLAP

Row 1 (RS) Slip 1, k3, transfer these 4 stitches to waste yarn or a small stitch holder; [slip 1, k1], 16 times, turn; transfer remaining 34 stitches to waste yarn or another small stitch holder — 32 flap stitches.

Row 2 Slip 1, purl to end.

Working flap stitches only, repeat [Rows 1 and 2] 15 times — 32 flap rows.

HEEL TURN

Row 1 (RS) Slip 1, k18, ssk, k1, turn, leaving 10 stitches unworked.

Row 2 (WS) Slip 1, p7, p2tog, p1, turn, leaving 10 stitches unworked.

Row 3 Slip 1, knit to 1 stitch before gap formed on previous row, ssk [1 stitch from each side of gap], k1, turn.

Row 4 Slip 1, purl to 1 stitch before gap formed on previous row, p2tog [1 stitch from each side of gap], p1, turn.

Repeat Rows 3 and 4 until all heel stitches have been worked, ending with a WS row — 20 heel stitches remain.

GUSSET

Row 1 (RS) Knit to end of heel; pick up and knit 16 stitches along the side of the flap, place marker; work across 34 stitches from holder maintaining established pattern and color sequence.

Row 2 Slip 1, purl to end of heel; pick up and purl [from the back of the stitch] 16 stitches along the side of the flap, place marker; p4 from holder — 90 stitches.

Row 3 Maintaining established pattern, slip 1, work to marker, k1, ssk, knit to 3 stitches before next marker, k2tog, k1, work to end — 88 stitches.

Row 4 Slip 1, purl to end.

Repeat [Rows 3 and 4] 9 times — 70 stitches. Remove markers.

FOOT

Work even in established patterns until foot measures 7" from back of heel, or 2¼" shorter than desired length, ending with a WS row.

Coffee Break

Decrease Row (RS) Slip 1, knit to the end of the MC section; maintaining color sequence, decrease across each Lace section as follows: [k1, yo, ssk twice, k2tog twice, yo, k1] 3 times — 64 stitches.

Work 1 row even. Cut A, B, and C.

With MC, work 2 rows in stockinette stitch.

ROUND TOE

Setup Row (RS) Slip 1, k5, k2tog, place marker, *k6, k2tog, place marker; repeat from * to end — 56 stitches.

Work 5 rows even.

Decrease Row (RS) Slip 1, *knit to 2 stitches before marker, k2tog, repeat from * to end — 48 stitches.

Repeat Decrease Row every 6th row twice, every 4th row once, then every RS row once, ending with a WS row — 16 stitches.

Next Row Slip 1, k1, [k2tog] 7 times — 9 stitches.

Last Row Slip 1, p6, ssp — 8 stitches.

Measure the yarn out to about five times the length of the sock and cut. Using a yarn needle, thread the tail through all stitches and pull tight. Don't cut the yarn yet; the rest is used for seaming.

SEAM

Fold the sock with wrong sides together. Match up the slipped edge stitches and pin in place. Using the crochet hook, slip stitch knitwise from the front into each corresponding set of stitches up to the top of the cuff to close the seam. (See page 15.)

Fasten off. Weave in ends. Block as desired.

Coffee Break

Right Sock

Work Cuff as for Left Sock.

LEG

Setup Row (RS) Cut MC; slipping the first stitch, work the 10-stitch Lace pattern 8 times across the row in the following color sequence: 1 repeat each with A, B, C; 5 repeats with MC.

Slipping the first stitch of every row, work 13 rows in established Lace pattern and color sequence.

Decrease Row (RS) Slipping the first stitch of the row, work 30 stitches in established Lace pattern and color sequence; with MC, [k1, yo, ssk twice, k2tog twice, yo, k1] 5 times — 70 stitches.

Working all MC stitches in stockinette stitch and other colors in established Lace pattern, work even until sock measures 5" or desired length.

HEEL FLAP

Row 1 (RS) Work 30 stitches in established pattern, k4 with MC, transfer 34 stitches just worked to waste yarn or a small stitch holder; [slip 1, k1] 16 times, turn; transfer remaining 4 stitches to waste yarn or another small stitch holder — 32 flap stitches.

Row 2 (WS) Slip 1, purl to end.

Complete Heel Flap and Heel Turn as for Left Sock.

GUSSET

Row 1 (RS) Knit to end of heel; pick up and knit 16 stitches along the side of the flap, place marker; k4 from holder.

Row 2 Slip 1, purl to end of heel; pick up and purl [from the back of the stitch] 16 stitches along the side of the flap, place marker; p34 from holder, maintaining the established pattern and color sequence — 90 stitches.

Complete Gusset and Leg as for Left Sock, ending before Decrease Row.

Decrease Row (RS) Maintaining color sequence, decrease across each lace section as follows: Slip 1, yo, ssk twice, k2tog twice, yo, k1, [k1, yo, ssk twice, k2tog twice, yo, k1] twice; knit to end of MC section — 64 stitches.

Next Row With MC, slip 1, p39, cut MC; maintaining color sequence, p23; rejoin MC here and p1. Cut A, B, and C.

With MC, work 2 rows in stockinette stitch.

Work Round Toe as for Left Sock.

SEAM

Work as for Left Sock, but slip stitch purlwise from the back to close the seam.

Coffee Break

110

Winter Delights:
Gingerbread Men and Snowmen

These two Guernsey-style socks
with touches of color are both celebrations of
winter. Pink frosting and tiny twists of stitches
become little gingerbread men dancing around the
ankle. A variation iced in blue transforms tiny cables
into little snowmen standing guard around the ankle.
Because of the different patterns, there will be changes
in the stitch count as you go.

111

SIZES	Woman M (L)
FINISHED MEASUREMENTS	Circumference: 7 (8)" Foot length: 9 (10)"
YARN	Cascade Heritage, fingering weight, 75% superwash merino wool / 25% nylon, 437 yds / 100 g Gingerbread Men: 1 skein Sunflower #5643 (MC) and 43 yds Tutu #5613 (CC) Snowmen: 1 skein Snow #5618 (MC) and 43 yds Baby Blue #5651 (CC)
NEEDLES	US 0 (2.0 mm) 9" straight needles *or size needed to obtain gauge*
OTHER SUPPLIES	Stitch markers, waste yarn or small stitch holders, yarn needle, seaming pins, US F/5 (3.75 mm) crochet hook *or size needed to match the slipped edge stitches* (see Closing the Seam, page 15)
GAUGE	36 stitches and 48 rows = 4" in stockinette stitch Knit a swatch for accurate sizing.

Chevron [multiple of 12 (14) stitches + 1]

Row 1 (RS) With MC, slip 1 purlwise, ssk, k3 (4), inc 1 using e-wrap method, k1, inc 1, k3 (4), k2tog, k1, repeat from * to end.

Row 2 Slip 1, *k5 (6), p1; repeat from * to end.

Row 3 With CC, slip 1 purlwise, *ssk, k3 (4), inc 1, slip 1, inc 1, k3 (4), k2tog, slip 1; repeat from *, ending last repeat with k1.

Row 4 Slip 1, *k5 (6), slip 1 wyif; repeat from *, ending last repeat with p1.

Repeat Rows 1–4 for pattern.

Mistake Stitch Rib

Row 1 Slip 1, k4 (5), p1, knit to last 6 (7) stitches, p1, k5 (6).

Row 2 Slip 1, p4 (5), k1, *p1, k1; repeat from * to last 6 (7) stitches, k1, p5 (6).

Row 3 Slip 1, k0 (1), p2, k2, p1, knit to last 6 (7) stitches, p1, k2, p2, k1 (2).

Row 4 Slip 1, p0 (1), k2, p2, k1, *p1, k1; repeat from * to last 6 (7) stitches, k1, p2, k2, p1 (2).

Repeat Rows 1–4 for pattern.

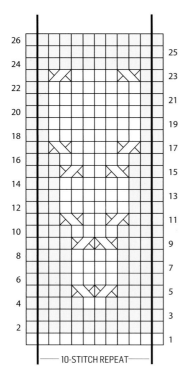

SNOWMEN CHART

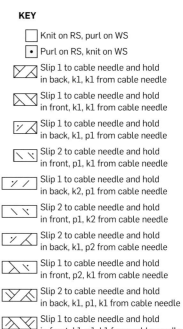

BOXES CHART

KEY

☐ Knit on RS, purl on WS

• Purl on RS, knit on WS

⬚ Slip 1 to cable needle and hold in back, k1, k1 from cable needle

⬚ Slip 1 to cable needle and hold in front, k1, k1 from cable needle

⬚ Slip 1 to cable needle and hold in back, k1, p1 from cable needle

⬚ Slip 2 to cable needle and hold in front, p1, k1 from cable needle

⬚ Slip 1 to cable needle and hold in back, k2, p1 from cable needle

⬚ Slip 2 to cable needle and hold in front, p1, k2 from cable needle

⬚ Slip 2 to cable needle and hold in back, k1, p2 from cable needle

⬚ Slip 1 to cable needle and hold in front, p2, k1 from cable needle

⬚ Slip 2 to cable needle and hold in back, k1, p1, k1 from cable needle

⬚ Slip 1 to cable needle and hold in front, k1, p1, k1 from cable needle

Gingerbread Men and Snowmen

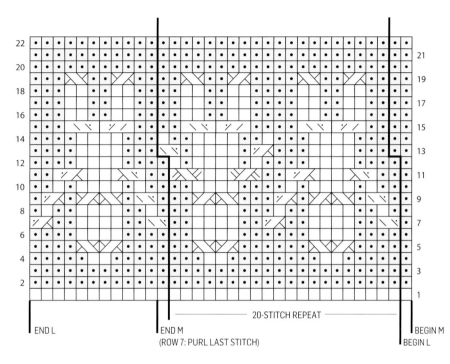

GINGERBREAD MEN CHART

Pattern Notes

- These socks are designed with a round heel and a round toe.
- Both versions are worked the same except for the Snowmen and Gingerbread Men chart inserts on the leg, each of which requires a different stitch count.
- Gusset stitches are picked up with CC before the heel is turned in order to frame the heel with a garter stripe in CC. The gusset is continued after the heel turn.
- Don't forget to slip the first stitch of every row purlwise. This is vital to achieving a smooth seam.

Left Sock

CUFF

With CC, cast on 73 (85) stitches loosely.

Join MC, but do not cut CC.

Starting with MC and alternating CC as described, work 10 rows in Chevron pattern, ending with Row 2. Cut CC yarn but continue work in MC.

Placing markers after first 5 (6) stitches and before last 5 (6) stitches on first row, work 10 rows in Mistake Stitch Rib, ending with Row 2.

> **Note** The knit rib lines should line up with the downward-pointing slipped stitches of the Chevron pattern.

LEG

Cut a strand of MC about 30" long to use at end of row. This will provide enough for area at ends of both CC stripes.

Gingerbread Men Version

Stripe Row 1 With MC, slip 1, k0 (1), p2, k2; join CC and knit to last 5 (6) stitches; join strand of MC, k2, p2, k1 (2).

Stripe Row 2 With MC, slip 1, p0 (1), k2, p2, cut strand of MC; with CC, decrease 0 (1) stitch, then knit to last 5 (6) stitches; with MC, p2, k2, p1 (2) — 73 (84) stitches. Cut CC.

Maintaining the first and last 5 (6) stitches in the established pattern, work the Gingerbread Men Chart across the center 63 (72) stitches, decreasing 1 (6) stitch(es) evenly across the last row — 72 (78) stitches.

Gingerbread Men and Snowmen

Snowmen Version

Stripe Row 1 With MC, slip 1, k0 (1), p2, k2; join CC and knit to last 5 (6) stitches; with strand of MC, k2, p2, k1 (2).

Stripe Row 2 With MC, slip 1, p0 (1), k2, p2, cut MC; with CC, decrease 1 stitch, then knit to last 5 (6) stitches; with MC, p2, k2, p1 (2) — 72 (84) stitches. Cut CC.

Maintaining the first and last 5 (6) stitches in the established pattern, work the Snowmen Chart across the center 62 (72) stitches, decreasing 0 (6) stitches evenly across the last row — 72 (78) stitches.

Both Versions

Repeat Stripe Rows 1 and 2, but do not decrease — 72 (78) stitches.

Maintaining the first and last 5 (6) stitches in the established pattern, work the Boxes Chart across the center 62 (66) stitches.

> **Note** Size S will be one block (4 stitches) short of a full repeat.

Repeat Stripe Rows 1 and 2, but increase 0 (1) stitch on Row 2 — 72 (79) stitches.

HEEL FLAP

Row 1 (RS) With MC, slip 1, k4 (5), transfer these 5 (6) stitches to waste yarn or a small stitch holder; k36 (39), turn; transfer remaining 31 (34) stitches to waste yarn or another small stitch holder — 36 (39) flap stitches.

Row 2 Slip 1, k4 (3), *p1, k4 (5); repeat from * to last 6 (5) stitches, p1, k5 (4).

Row 3 With CC, slip 1, k4 (3), *slip 1, k4 (5); repeat from * to last 6 (5) stitches, slip 1, k5 (4).

Row 4 Slip 1, k4 (3), *slip 1 wyif, k4 (5); repeat from * to last 6 (5) stitches, slip 1 wyif, k5 (4).

Working flap stitches only, repeat [Rows 1–4] 8 times, then work Rows 1 and 2, increasing 0 (1) stitch on the last row — 38 flap rows and 36 (40) stitches.

HEEL FLAP STRIPE

Follow the next set of instructions carefully. The gusset stitches are picked up before turning the heel to enclose the heel flap within a CC frame.

Row 1 (RS) With CC, k36 (40) across heel flap; pick up and knit 19 (20) stitches along the side of the flap, then pick up 1 extra stitch in CC row below.

117

Gingerbread Men and Snowmen

Row 2 Knit to the end of the heel flap; pick up and purl [from the back of the stitch] 19 (20) stitches along the side of the heel flap, then pick up 1 extra stitch in CC row below — 76 (82) stitches.

Row 3 P20 (21); cut CC.

Transfer 20 (21) gusset stitches on each side of the heel to waste yarn or a stitch holder — 36 (40) heel stitches remain. Continue with MC only to the end of the sock.

HEEL TURN

Row 1 (RS) Slip 1, k20 (22), ssk, k1, turn, leaving 12 (14) stitches unworked.

Row 2 (WS) Slip 1, p7, p2tog, p1, turn, leaving 12 (14) stitches unworked.

Row 3 Slip 1, knit to 1 stitch before gap formed on previous row, ssk [1 stitch from each side of gap], k1, turn.

Row 4 Slip 1, purl to 1 stitch before gap formed on previous row, p2tog [1 stitch from each side of gap], p1, turn.

Repeat Rows 3 and 4 until all heel stitches have been worked, ending with a WS row — 22 (24) heel stitches remain.

GUSSET

Row 1 (RS) Slip 1, knit to end of heel; k18 (19) gusset stitches, k2tog, place marker; k31 (34) from holder.

Row 2 Slip 1, purl to marker; purl to end of heel turn; p18 (19) gusset stitches, p2tog, place marker; p5 (6) from holder — 96 (104) stitches.

Row 3 Slip 1, k0 (1), p2, k2, slip marker; k1, ssk, knit to 3 stitches before next marker, k2tog, k1, slip marker; p2 (0), [k2, p2] 7 (8) times, k1 (2) — 94 (102) stitches.

Row 4 Slip 1, k0 (1), [p2, k2] 7 (8) times, p2 (0), slip marker; purl to next marker, p2, k2, p1 (2).

Maintaining the established 4-row pattern on the instep/seam stitches and working stockinette stitch between the markers, decrease as on Row 3 every RS row 11 times — 72 (80) stitches.

FOOT

Slipping the first stitch of every row, work even in established pattern until foot measures 7 (8)" from the back of the heel, or about 2" shorter than desired length.

ROUND TOE

Setup Row (RS) Slip 1, k5, k2tog, place marker, *k6, k2tog, place marker; repeat from * to end — 63 (70) stitches.

Work 5 rows even.

Decrease Row Slip 1, *knit to 2 stitches before marker, k2tog; repeat from * to end — 54 (60) stitches.

Repeat Decrease Row every 6th row twice, every 4th row once, then every RS row once, ending with a WS row — 18 (20) stitches.

Next Row Slip 1, k1, k2tog 8 (9) times — 10 (11) stitches.

Last Row Slip 1, p7 (8), ssp — 9 (10) stitches.

Measure the yarn out to about five times the length of sock and cut. Using a yarn needle, thread the tail through all stitches and pull tight. Don't cut the yarn yet; the rest is used for seaming.

SEAM

Fold the sock with wrong sides together. Match up the slipped edge stitches and pin in place. Using the crochet hook, slip stitch knitwise from the front into each corresponding set of stitches up to the top of the cuff to close the seam. (See page 15.)

Fasten off. Weave in ends. Block as desired.

Right Sock

Work as for Left Sock to Heel Flap.

HEEL FLAP

Row 1 (RS) With MC, slip 1, k30 (33), transfer these stitches to waste yarn or a small stitch holder; k36 (39), turn; transfer

remaining 5 (6) stitches to waste yarn or another small stitch holder — 36 (39) flap stitches.

Continue as for Left Sock to Gusset.

GUSSET

Row 1 (RS) Slip 1, knit to end of heel; k18 (19) gusset stitches, k2tog, place marker; k5 (6) from holder.

Row 2 Slip 1, purl to marker; purl to end of heel turn; p18 (19) gusset stitches, p2tog, place marker; p31 (34) from holder — 96 (104) stitches.

Row 3 Slip 1, k0 (1), [p2, k2] 7 (8) times, p2 (0), slip marker; k1, ssk, knit to 3 stitches before next marker, k2tog, k1, slip marker; p2 (0), k2, p2, k1 (2) — 94 (102) stitches.

Row 4 Slip 1, p0 (1), k2, p2, slip marker; purl to next marker, k0 (2), [p2, k2] 7 (8) times, p1 (2).

Continue as for Left Sock until Round Toe is complete.

SEAM

Work as for Left Sock but slip stitch purlwise from the back to close the seam.

Gingerbread Men and Snowmen

119

Garden Trellis Argyle

I love to take walks and look at other gardeners' yards for ideas, and I'm often attracted by the colorful vines growing on a trellis by a porch. This sock is my nod to the skills of the gardener and my take on a classic argyle; the two seem a natural fit.

SIZES	Adult S (M, L)
FINISHED MEASUREMENTS	Circumference: 8 (9, 10)" Foot length: 8½ (9½, 10½)"
YARN	Cascade Heritage, fingering weight, 75% superwash merino wool / 25% nylon, 437 yds / 100 g, 1 skein each Citron #5629 (A), Moss #5612 (B), and Dark Plum #5632 (C), and about 10 yds of bright yellow yarn
NEEDLES	US 1 (2.25 mm) 9" straight needles *or size needed to obtain gauge*
OTHER SUPPLIES	Five bobbins for yarn colors (optional), waste yarn or small stitch holders, two stitch markers, yarn needle, pins, US F/5 (3.75 mm) crochet hook *or size needed to match the slipped edge stitches* (see Closing the Seam, page 15)
GAUGE	32 stitches and 40 rows = 4" in stockinette stitch Knit a swatch for accurate sizing.

Pattern Notes

- This sock is designed with a round heel and round toe.

- The cuff is worked with two-color corrugated ribbing. To avoid puckering, carry the yarn not in use loosely across the wrong side.

- The colorwork for this sock is worked using a combination of stranded and intarsia methods. Use a separate ball or bobbin for each section worked in yarn C. Work yarn A all the way across. Use shorter lengths of yarn B for the diagonals as indicated on the chart. When changing colors, drop old color and pick up new color from under old color to link the yarns and prevent holes.

- Don't forget to slip the first stitch of every row purlwise. This is vital to achieving a smooth seam.

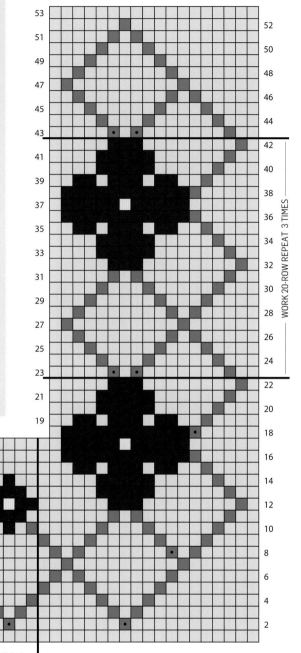

WORK 20-ROW REPEAT 3 TIMES

WORK 10-STITCH REPEAT
3 (4, 5) TIMES

LEFT SOCK CHART

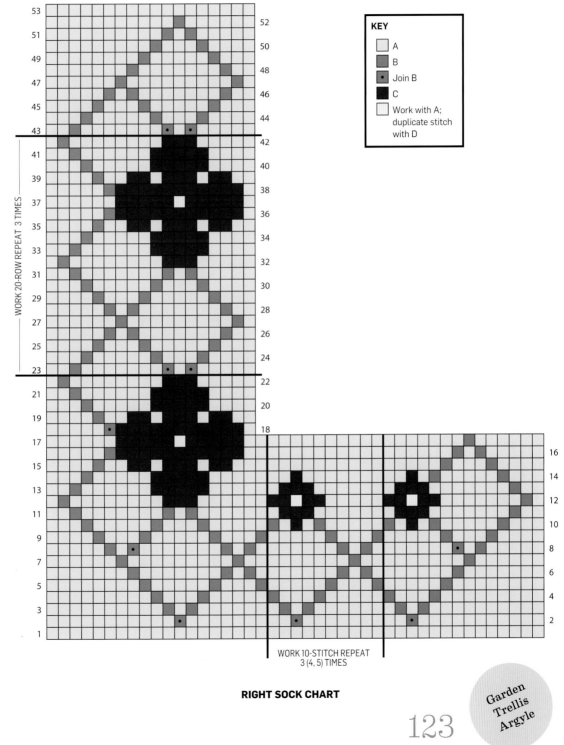

KEY

- A
- B
- • Join B
- C
- Work with A; duplicate stitch with D

WORK 20-ROW REPEAT 3 TIMES

WORK 10-STITCH REPEAT
3 (4, 5) TIMES

RIGHT SOCK CHART

123

Garden Trellis Argyle

Left Sock

CUFF

> **Note** Corrugated ribbing is a two-color stranded ribbing with one color knitted and the other color purled. Keep the floats loose on the wrong side so as not to pucker your work.

With A, cast on 63 (73, 83) stitches loosely.

Row 1 (RS) Slip 1, *p1 B, k1 A, repeat from * to last stitch, k1 A.

Slipping the first stitch of every row, work in established two-color rib until piece measures 1½", ending with a RS row. Cut B.

LEG

Cut 6 strands of B about 36" long.

Row 1 (WS) With A, slip 1, purl to end [Garden Trellis Chart Row 1].

Row 2 (RS) Work Garden Trellis Chart Row 2 as follows: Slip 1, knit to first B square [marked with a dot], insert needle into next stitch on needle, fold one 36" strand of B in half and, from the RS, draw a loop of B through the stitch. Let the ends hang down the back freely. (On the next row, one end will be used for right diagonal and the other for the left — two fewer ends to work in where joined.) Continue across the row, adding a new strand of B for any short diagonals at cells marked with a dot on the chart.

Rows 3–17 Slipping the first stitch of every row, work chart to Row 17.

Row 18 (RS) Continuing the chart down the side of leg and working all other stitches with A, decrease only the XL 2 stitches — 63 (73, 81) stitches.

Rows 19–51 Slipping the first stitch of every row, work even following the chart, ending with Row 31 of the chart [9th row of 20-row repeat].

HEEL FLAP

> **Note** Do not slip the first stitch of each row for Flap. Just knit or purl the beginning of each heel flap row as normal.

Row 1 (RS) Slip 1, k1, transfer these 2 stitches to waste yarn or a small stitch holder; with A, *k1, [p1 B, k1 A] 15 (18, 20) times, turn; transfer remaining 28 (34, 38) stitches to waste yarn or another small stitch holder — 31 (37, 41) flap stitches.

Row 2 With A p1, [k1 B, p1 A] 15 (18, 20) times, turn.

Working the flap stitches only, repeat [Rows 1 and 2] 8 (9, 10) times — 18 (22, 24) flap rows. Cut B.

Garden Trellis Argyle

HEEL TURN

Row 1 (RS) With A, slip 1, k8 (10, 12), k2tog, k7 (9, 9), ssk, k1, turn, leaving 10 (12, 14) stitches unworked.

Row 2 (WS) Slip 1, p5 (7, 7), p2tog, p1, turn, leaving 10 (12, 14) stitches unworked.

Row 3 Slip 1, knit to 1 stitch before gap formed on previous row, ssk [1 stitch from each side of gap], k1, turn.

Row 4 Slip 1, purl to 1 stitch before gap formed on previous row, p2tog [1 stitch from each side of gap], p1, turn.

Repeat Rows 3 and 4 until all heel stitches have been worked, ending with a WS row — 18 (22, 24) heel stitches remain.

GUSSET

Row 1 (RS) Knit to end of heel; pick up and knit 16 (18, 20) stitches evenly along the side of the flap, place marker; work in established pattern across 30 (34, 38) stitches on holder.

Row 2 Slip 1, work in pattern to marker; purl to end of heel; pick up and purl 16 (18, 20) stitches evenly along the side of the flap, place marker; work 2 stitches from holder — 80 (94, 104) stitches.

Row 3 Slip 1, k1, slip marker, k1, ssk, knit to 3 stitches before next marker, k2tog, k1, slip marker, work in established pattern to end — 80 (92, 102) sts.

Row 4 Slip 1, work as established to end.

Repeat [Rows 3 and 4] 8 (10, 11) times — 64 (72, 80) stitches. Remove markers.

FOOT

Slipping the first stitch of every row and continuing the charted color pattern until complete, and then continuing with A only, work in stockinette stitch until foot measures about 6½ (7½, 8½)" from the back of the heel, or about 2" shorter than desired length.

ROUND TOE

Setup Row (RS) Slip 1, k5, k2tog, place marker, *k6, k2tog, place marker, repeat to end — 56 (63, 70) sts.

Continuing in stockinette stitch, work 5 rows even.

Decrease Row (RS) Slip 1, *knit to 2 stitches before marker, k2tog, slip marker, repeat from * to end — 48 (54, 60) stitches.

Repeat Decrease Row every 6th row twice, every 4th row once, then every RS row once, ending with a WS row — 116 (18, 20) stitches.

Garden Trellis Argyle

Next Row Slip 1, k1, k2tog 7 (8, 9) times — 9 (10, 11) stitches.

Last Row Slip 1, p6 (7, 8), ssp — 8 (9, 10) stitches.

Measure the yarn out to about five times the length of sock and cut. Using a yarn needle, thread the tail through all stitches and pull up tight. Don't cut the yarn yet; the rest is used for seaming.

SEAM

Fold the sock with wrong sides together. Match up the slipped edge stitches and pin in place. Using the crochet hook, slip stitch knitwise from the front into each corresponding set of stitches up to the top of the cuff to close the seam. (See page 15.)

Fasten off. Weave in ends.

Right Sock

Following Left Sock Chart, work as for Right Sock to Heel Flap.

HEEL FLAP

Note Do not slip the first stitch of each row for Flap. Just knit or purl the beginning of each heel flap row as normal.

Row 1 (RS) Slip 1, work 27 (33, 37) stitches following the chart, then transfer to waste yarn or a small stitch holder; with A *k1, [p1 B, k1 A] 15 (18, 20) times, turn; transfer remaining 2 stitches to waste yarn or another small stitch holder — 31 (37, 41) stitches.

Row 2 With A p1, [k1 B, p1 A] 15 (18, 20) times, turn.

Complete Heel Flap and Heel Turn as for Left Sock.

GUSSET

Row 1 (RS) Knit to the end of the heel; pick up and knit 16 (18, 20) stitches along the side of the flap, place marker; work 2 stitches from the holder.

Row 2 Slip 1, work in pattern to marker; purl to end of heel; pick up and purl [from the back of the stitch] 16 (18, 20) stitches along the side of the flap, place marker; work in established pattern across 28 (34, 38) stitches on holder — 80 (94, 104) stitches.

Continue as for Left Sock, until Round Toe is complete.

SEAM

Work as for Left Sock, but slip stitch purlwise from the back to close the seam. Block as desired.

Touch Me Not

Just as a touch-me-not seed pod flips itself out to propel its seeds when disturbed, this sock shakes things up and turns things inside out in reverse stockinette stitch. A leafy lace pattern straddles the seam down the front of the sock and a complementary lace cuff resembling seed pods extends down the back of the leg and heel.

SIZE	Woman M
FINISHED MEASUREMENTS	Circumference: 7" Foot length: 9½"
YARN	Cascade Yarns Heritage, fingering weight, 75% superwash merino wool / 25% nylon, 437 yds / 100 g, 1 skein Primavera #5659
NEEDLES	US 1 (2.25 mm) 9" straight needles *or size needed to obtain gauge*
OTHER SUPPLIES	Waste yarn or stitch holders, two stitch markers, yarn needle, seaming pins, US F/5 (3.75 mm) crochet hook, *or size needed to match the longer slipped edge stitches* (see Closing the Seam, page 15)
GAUGE	32 stitches and 44 rows = 4" in reverse stockinette stitch Knit a swatch for accurate sizing.

Special Abbreviation

M1P (Make 1 Purlwise) Insert left-hand needle from front to back under the bar between the last stitch worked and next stitch on left-hand needle. With right-hand needle, purl into the back of this loop.

Pattern Notes

- This sock is designed with a round heel and wedge toe. The seam is at center front, so left and right socks are worked the same.

- The lace panel charts show two repeats of the pattern. The last full leaf repeat is worked while shaping the toe. Work Rows 1–28, then repeat Rows 15–28 throughout the leg and foot until beginning the toe shaping on Row 22. The toe decreases gradually eliminate the purl stitches at the inner edges of the leaf.

- Don't forget to slip the first stitch of every row purlwise. This is vital to achieving a smooth seam.

KEY

☐	Knit on RS, purl on WS
•	Purl on RS, knit on WS
V	Slip 1 purlwise
O	Yo
╱	K2tog
╲	Ssk
⋏	K3tog
⋋	Sssk
⦷	M1 purlwise
╲	Leg and Foot: P on RS, k on WS Toe: Ssk
╱	Leg and Foot: P on RS, k on WS Toe: K2tog
•	Leg and Foot: P on RS, k on WS Toe: No stitch
☐	No stitch
⧄	Slip 1 to cable needle and hold in front, p1, k1 from cable needle
⧄	Slip 1 to cable needle and hold in back, k1, p1 from cable needle

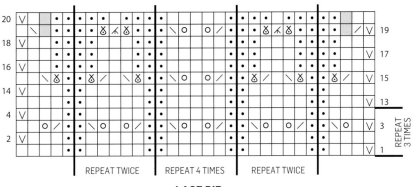

LACE RIB

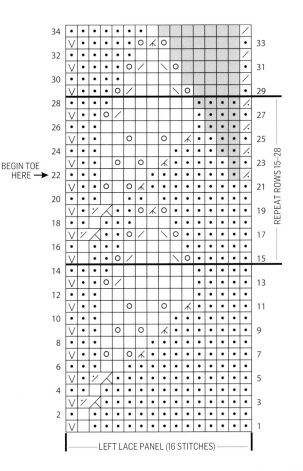

LEFT LACE PANEL (16 STITCHES)

BEGIN TOE HERE →

REPEAT ROWS 15–28

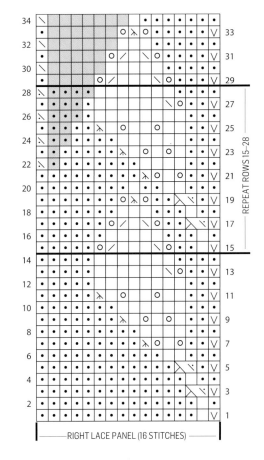

RIGHT LACE PANEL (16 STITCHES)

REPEAT ROWS 15–28

LEAF LACE PANELS

129

Touch Me Not

Both Socks

CUFF

Cast on 66 stitches loosely.

Work the 20-row Lace Rib chart — 64 stitches at end of chart.

LEG

Setup Row (RS) Slipping the first stitch of every row, work the 16-stitch Right Lace Panel; continue established Lace Rib over center 32 stitches; then work the 16-stitch Left Lace Panel.

Work even until the piece measures 5" or desired length to the heel, ending with Row 4 of Lace Rib. Make a note of the last row of the Right and Left Lace Panels worked.

HEEL FLAP

Row 1 (RS) Slip 1, work 15 stitches in pattern and transfer to waste yarn or a stitch holder; work 32 stitches in established Lace Rib, turn; transfer remaining 16 stitches to waste yarn or another stitch holder — 32 flap stitches.

Rows 2–22 Slipping the first stitch of every row, work in established Lace Rib.

Row 23 Slip 1, *p2, M1P, ssk, k1, k2tog, M1P; repeat from * to last 3 stitches, p3.

Rows 24 Slip 1 and work even in established Lace Rib, knitting the knit stitches and purling the purl stitches.

Row 25 Slip 1, *p3, M1P, k3tog, M1P, p1; repeat from * to last 3 stitches, p3.

Row 26 Slip 1, *k4, p1, k2; repeat from * to last 3 stitches, k3.

Rows 27–32 Work even in reverse stockinette stitch.

HEEL TURN

Row 1 (RS) Slip 1, p18, p2tog, p1, turn, leaving 10 stitches unworked.

Row 2 (WS) Slip 1, k7, ssk, k1, turn, leaving 10 stitches unworked.

Row 3 Slip 1, purl to 1 stitch before gap formed on previous row, p2tog [1 stitch from each side of gap], k1, turn.

Row 4 Slip 1, knit to 1 stitch before gap formed on previous row, ssk [1 stitch from each side of gap], k1, turn.

Repeat Rows 3 and 4 until all heel stitches have been worked, ending with a WS row — 20 heel stitches remain.

GUSSET

Row 1 (RS) Slip 1, purl to the end of the heel; pick up and knit 16 stitches along the side of the flap, place marker; after referring to notes for last row worked of Left Lace Panel, resume pattern across 16 stitches from holder.

Row 2 Slip 1, work to the end of the heel; pick up and purl 16 stitches along the side of the flap, place marker; after referring to notes for last row worked of Right Lace Panel, resume pattern across 16 stitches from holder — 84 stitches.

Row 3 Slip 1, work in pattern to marker, purl to next marker, work in pattern to end of row.

Row 4 (WS) Slip 1, work in pattern to marker, ssk, knit to 2 stitches before next marker, k2tog, work in pattern to end of row — 82 stitches.

Repeat [Rows 3 and 4] 9 times — 64 stitches. Leave markers on the needle.

FOOT

Slipping the first stitch of every row, continue working the Right and Left Lace Panel pattern on the first and last 16 stitches and work the center 32 stitches in reverse stockinette stitch. Work even until the foot measures approximately 7" from the back of the heel, or about 2" shorter than desired length, ending with Row 21 of the Right and Left Lace Panels.

WEDGE TOE

Row 1 (WS) Work in pattern to 2 stitches before marker, k2tog, ssk, knit to 2 stitches before marker, k2tog, ssk, work in pattern to end — 60 stitches.

Row 2 Work even.

Repeat [Rows 1 and 2] 7 times. After the Right and Left Lace Panel pattern is complete, work all stitches in reverse stockinette to the end of the toe — 32 stitches.

Row 3 (WS) Slip 1, *knit to 2 stitches before marker, k2tog, ssk; repeat from * once, knit to end of row — 28 stitches.

Row 4 Slip 1, *purl to 2 stitches before marker, ssp, p2tog; repeat from * once, purl to end of row — 24 stitches.

Repeat Rows 3 and 4 twice, then work 1 WS row even — 8 stitches.

Measure the yarn out to about five times the length of sock and cut. Using a yarn needle, thread the tail through all stitches and pull tight. Don't cut the yarn yet; the rest is used for seaming.

SEAM

Fold the sock with wrong sides together. Match up the slipped edge stitches and pin in place. Using the crochet hook, slip stitch (knitwise from the front for left sock; purlwise from the back for right sock) into each corresponding set of stitches up to top of cuff to close seam. (See page 15.)

Fasten off. Weave in ends. Block as desired.

Carnegie Hall

Whether you have plans for an evening out or just feel like listening to music at home, dress your feet up in style. This design calls for some very simple crochet shells along the edge of the "shirt," set off by a bow tie and tiny little buttons. Both socks are identical, with a center front seam.

SIZE	Woman M
FINISHED MEASUREMENTS	Circumference: 7" Foot length: 9"
YARN	Deborah Norville Collection Serenity Sock Weight, fingering weight, 25% rayon from bamboo/50% superwash merino/25% nylon, 230 yds/50 g, 2 skeins Black #12 (MC) and 1 skein Soft White #01 (CC)
NEEDLES	US 1 (2.25 mm) 9" straight needles *or size needed to obtain gauge*
OTHER SUPPLIES	Two or three bobbins for yarn colors (optional), four stitch markers, cable needle, waste yarn or stitch holders, yarn needle, seaming pins, US F/5 (3.75 mm) crochet hook *or size needed to match the longer slipped edge stitches* (see Closing the Seam, page 15), six ¼" black buttons (doll buttons are good), sewing needle and thread
GAUGE	36 stitches and 44 rows = 4" in stockinette stitch Knit a swatch for accurate sizing.

Special Abbreviations

Dec CC / Inc MC Slip 1 CC to cable needle and hold in back, slip last CC stitch; transfer stitch on cable back to left-hand needle, then with MC, k2tog; work lifted increase in stitch below stitch just worked (p1 in stitch below on first row, k1 in stitch below in all other rows).

Inc MC / Dec CC With MC, work lifted increase in stitch below next stitch (p1 in stitch below on first row, k1 in stitch below in all other rows), slip last MC stitch knitwise; slip 1 CC stitch to cable needle and hold in front, slip next CC stitch knitwise, then with MC, knit slipped MC and CC stitches together (ssk); transfer stitch on cable needle to right-hand needle.

T2L (Twist 2 Left) Knit into the back loop of the 2nd stitch on the left-hand needle, then knit the first stitch; remove both stitches at the same time.

T2R (Twist 2 Right) Knit the 2nd stitch on the left-hand needle, then knit the first stitch; remove both stitches at the same time.

Mini-Cable Rib (multiple of 3+1)

Row 1 (RS) Slip 1, p1, *T2R, p1; repeat from * to last stitch, k1.
Rows 2 and 4 Slip 1, k1, *p2, k1; repeat from * to last stitch, p1.
Row 3 Slip 1, p1, *T2L, p1; repeat from * to last stitch, k1.
Repeat Rows 1–4 for pattern.

Pattern Notes

- This sock is designed with a round heel and wedge toe. The seam is at center front, so left and right socks are worked the same.

- The colorwork for this sock is worked using the intarsia method. Use a separate ball or bobbin of yarn for each color section. When changing colors, drop the old color and pick up the new color from under the old color to link the yarns and prevent holes.

- Don't forget to slip the first stitch of every row purlwise. This is vital to achieving a smooth seam.

Both Socks

CUFF

Cast on 78 stitches loosely in the following order: 16 stitches CC, 46 stitches MC, 16 stitches CC.

Maintaining color sequence, work 12 rows in Mini-Cable Rib.

LEG

Row 1 (RS) With CC, slip 1, [k2, slip 1] 5 times; with MC, work 7 stitches in

established Mini-Cable Rib, place marker, knit to last 7 MC stitches at the same time decreasing 2 stitches evenly across, place marker, work 7 stitches in established Mini-Cable Rib; with CC, [slip 1, k2] 5 times, k1 — 76 stitches with 44 MC stitches.

Rows 2, 4, and 6 Maintaining the color sequence, slip 1, knit the knit stitches and purl the purl stitches.

Row 3 Slip 1, work in the established slip-stitch pattern to last 2 CC stitches, Dec CC / Inc MC, work in established rib and stockinette stitch to last MC stitch, Inc MC / Dec CC, work to end of row in established slip-stitch pattern — 76 stitches, with 46 MC stitches and 15 CC stitches each side.

Row 5 Work even, maintaining the CC slipped-stitch pattern and 7-stitch Mini-Cable Rib panels, and working all other stitches in stockinette stitch.

Rows 7–56 Repeat [Rows 3–6] 12 times, then work Row 3 once more — 76 stitches, with 72 MC stitches and 2 CC stitches each side. Cut CC, leaving a tail about five times the length of the piece already worked.

Rows 57 and 58 With MC, work 2 rows even, maintaining the 7-stitch Mini-Cable Rib panels and working all other stitches in stockinette stitch.

HEEL FLAP

Row 1 (RS) Slip 1, k18, transfer these stitches to waste yarn or a stitch holder; slip 1, T2R, p1, [slip 1, k1] 6 times, slip 1, k2tog, [slip 1, k1] 7 times, slip 1, p1, T2R, p1, turn; transfer remaining 19 stitches to waste yarn or another stitch holder — 37 heel flap stitches.

Row 2 Slip 1, p2, k1, p29, k1, p2, k1.

Continuing to work Mini-Cable Rib at edges and slip-stitch pattern in center, work 36 more rows, increasing 1 stitch in the center of the last row — 38 stitches.

HEEL TURN

Row 1 (RS) Slip 1, k22, ssk, k1, turn, leaving 12 stitches unworked.

Row 2 (WS) Slip 1, p9, p2tog, p1, turn, leaving 12 stitches unworked.

Row 3 Slip 1, knit to 1 stitch before gap formed on previous row, ssk [1 stitch from each side of gap], k1, turn.

Row 4 Slip 1, purl to 1 stitch before gap formed on previous row, p2tog [1 stitch from each side of gap], p1, turn.

Repeat Rows 3 and 4 until all heel stitches have been worked, ending with a WS row — 24 heel stitches remain.

GUSSET

Row 1 (RS) Knit to the end of the heel, then pick up and knit 19 stitches along the side of the flap, place marker; work 19 stitches from holder, maintaining Mini-Cable Rib at sides.

Row 2 Slip 1, work in pattern to marker, purl to end of heel then pick up and purl [from the back of the stitch] 19 stitches along the side of the flap, place marker; work 19 stitches from holder, maintaining Mini-Cable Rib at sides — 100 stitches.

Row 3 Slip 1, work in established pattern to gusset marker, p1, ssk, knit to 3 stitches before next gusset marker, k2tog, p1, work in established pattern to end — 98 stitches.

Row 4 Slip 1, knit the knit stitches and purl the purl stitches.

Repeat [Rows 3 and 4] 11 times — 76 stitches. Remove markers.

FOOT

Slipping the first stitch of every row and maintaining the 4-stitch Mini-Cable Panel at the sides and all other stitches in stockinette stitch, work even until foot measures about 7½" from back of heel, or about 2" shorter than desired length, ending with a WS row.

WEDGE TOE

Setup Row (RS) Slip 1, k13, k2tog, place marker, work 6 stitches in established pattern including Mini-Cable Rib, place marker, ssk, k28, k2tog, place marker, work 6 stitches in established pattern including Mini-Cable Rib, place marker, ssk, k14 — 72 stitches.

Row 2 Slip 1, work even.

Row 3 Slip 1, *knit to 2 stitches before marker, k2tog, work 6 stitches in pattern, ssk; repeat from * once, knit to end — 68 stitches.

Row 4 Slip 1, work even.

Rows 5–17 Repeat [Rows 3 and 4] 6 times, then work Row 3 once more — 40 stitches.

Row 18 (WS) Slip 1, *purl to 2 stitches before marker, ssp, slip marker, work 6 stitches to next marker, slip marker, p2tog; repeat from * once, purl to end — 36 stitches.

Row 19 Slip 1, k3, k2tog, slip marker, p1, k2tog, p1, k2, slip marker, ssk, k8, k2tog, slip marker, k2, p1, k2tog, p1, slip marker, ssk, k4 — 30 stitches with 5 stitches between markers.

Row 20 Slip 1, p2, ssp, slip marker, k1, p1, k1, p2, slip marker, p2tog, k6, ssp, slip marker, p2, k1, p1, k1, slip marker, p2tog, p3 — 26 stitches with 5 stitches between markers,

Row 21 Slip 1, k1, k2tog, p2tog, p1, [ssk] twice, k4, [k2tog] twice, p1, p2tog, ssk, k2 — 18 stitches with 3 stitches between markers.

Row 22 Removing markers as you go, slip 1, ssp, k2, p1, p2tog, p2, ssp, p1, k2, p2tog, p1 — 14 stitches.

Carnegie Hall

Row 23 Slip 1, [k2tog] 6 times, k1 —
8 stitches.

Row 24 Slip 1, p7.

Measure the yarn out to about five times
the length of sock to the CC section and
cut. Using a yarn needle, thread the tail
through all stitches and pull tight. Don't cut
the yarn yet; the rest is used for seaming.

SEAM

Fold the sock with wrong sides together.
Match up the slipped edge stitches and
pin in place. Using the crochet hook, slip
stitch the seam (knitwise from the front
of seam for left sock, purlwise from the
back for right sock) into each corresponding set of stitches up to the top of the cuff
to close the seam, changing colors when
you get to the CC section. (See page 15.)

Optional: Since both socks are identical,
the seam could be worked the same way.

Fasten off. Weave in ends. Block as
desired.

FINISHING

Shirt Ruffle

Ruffle will be worked in diagonal slip-stitch
lines at the outer edge of the CC section.

With the crochet hook and CC section
facing you, join CC in first slipped stitch
below cuff.

*Slip st, skip 1, work 5 dc in next slip
stitch [1 shell made]; repeat from * to
bottom of point — 7 shells worked;
you may need to adjust slightly to fit
by skipping or not skipping an extra
stitch. (The "technical" term these days
is fudging.) Slip stitch in both bottom
stitches to turn the corner, then work
7 more shells along the other diagonal
line to the last slip stitch before the
cuff, ending with a slip stitch.

Cut yarn and fasten off. Weave in ends.

Bow Tie

With MC, cast on 11 stitches. Work in k1,
p1 rib for 1½", then bind off. Wrap yarn
around the center several times to gather
it into a bow. Weave in the ends. Sew to
the seam line just below the cuff.

Sew three small buttons evenly spaced to
front of "shirt" area. Block as desired.

Yarn used in these socks came from the following stores:

Angelika's Yarn Store
503-200-5991
www.yarn-store.com

Annie's
800-282-6643
www.anniescatalog.com

Berroco, Inc.
401-769-1212
www.berrocco.com

Cascade Yarns
www.cascadeyarns.com

Creatively Dyed Yarn
info@creativelydyed.net
http://creativelydyedyarn.com

Elsebeth Lavold Yarns
Knitting Fever, Inc.
516-546-3600
www.knittingfever.com/c/elsebeth-lavold/yarn

FatCatKnits
315-985-3131
http://stores.fatcatknits.com

Hobby Lobby
www.hobbylobby.com

Patons
888-368-8401
www.patonsyarns.com

Premier Yarns and Herrschners, Inc.
888-458-3588
www.premieryarns.com
Deborah Norville Yarn

Universal Yarn, Inc.
877-864-9276
www.universalyarn.com

Resources

Glossary

Far be it from me to try to define every knitting term out there. Instead I recommend some of the very good knitting references available for those learning to knit and for the serious knitter. This glossary will cover those terms that I have used in this book and that form a basis of basic knitting terminology. I have also included a few crochet terms that have been used.

cast on To form a foundation row of stitches from which to begin knitting.

CC contrasting yarn color

chain Begin with a slip knot on the crochet hook. Yarn over the hook and draw through the loop on the hook. Repeat for specified length or number of stitches.

dc (double crochet) With 1 stitch on the hook, wrap the yarn around the hook before inserting the hook in your work. Wrap and pull a loop through your work and the first wrap on the hook. Wrap yarn around the hook and pull through the second wrap and the stitch on hook.

decrease To remove a stitch by various techniques specified:

k2tog This is the usual method of decreasing 1 stitch if not directly specified in the instructions. Insert the needle into 2 stitches and knit together at the same time. This makes a right-leaning decrease.

ssk Decrease 1 stitch by slipping 1 stitch knitwise, slipping another stitch knitwise, and then inserting the left-hand needle into the front of both stitches on the right-hand needle and knitting them together at the same time. This makes a left-leaning decrease.

p2tog Decrease 1 stitch on the wrong (purl) side by purling 2 stitches together at the same time. In stockinette stitch, this makes a right-leaning decrease on the right (knit) side.

ssp To decrease 1 stitch on what is usually the wrong (purl) side, slip 1 stitch knitwise, slip another stitch knitwise, and then slide both stitches back to the left-hand needle together. Insert the tip of the right-hand needle around to the back left side of both stitches and purl them both together at the same time. This makes a left-leaning decrease on the knit side (most often the right side). It may feel a bit awkward, but it's very useful.

g gram(s)

increase To add a stitch by various techniques specified.

k1fb Increase 1 stitch by knitting into the front leg of a stitch and then, without taking it off the left-hand needle, twisting around and knitting into the back leg of the stitch.

knit 1 below Increase 1 stitch by knitting into the stitch in the row below the stitches on the needle.

e-wrap Increase 1 stitch by wrapping the yarn around your right-hand thumb and placing the loop on the needle, so-called because it resembles the script letter *e*.

M1 (make one) Increase 1 stitch by lifting the bar between 2 stitches and knitting or purling into the back or front half of it to make a twisted stitch, which makes a tighter stitch and prevents a hole.

yo (yarn over) Increase 1 stitch by moving the yarn to the front between the needles before knitting the next stitch and then lifting the yarn over the needle to the back to continue knitting. This makes a visible space (or hole) in the knitting. It's often used in lace knitting.

Jeny's Surprisingly Stretchy Bind Off This bind-off throws in yarn-overs wrapped in different directions depending on whether you're knitting or purling. For detailed instructions, search for this bind off online at Knitty.com or see Leslie Ann Bestor's *Cast On, Bind Off*.

join To start using a new strand of yarn. There is no need to tie or knot the new piece, simply leave a long-enough tail so you can easily weave in the ends later. While holding the new strand next to your work, start knitting it in.

k knit

k2tog Knit 2 stitches together.

Kitchener stitch Here's how to work Kitchener stitch, also known as grafting or weaving the seam.

Cut the yarn long enough to complete the seam and to finish the end off on the inside.

Hold both needles alongside each other, wrong sides together, and thread the yarn onto a yarn needle.

Do not pull the stitches tight as you work, but try to match the size of the stitches in your knitting. You can adjust them after you're done.

Using the yarn needle, go into the stitch on the front needle as if to purl and pull the yarn all the way through. Leave the stitch on the needle.

Go into the stitch on the back needle as if to knit and pull the yarn all the way through. Leave the stitch on the needle.

*Go into the stitch on the front needle as if to knit, take it off the needle.

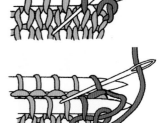

Go into the next stitch on the front needle as if to purl, leave it on the needle.

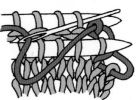

Go into the stitch on the back needle as if to purl, take it off.

Go into the next stitch on the back needle as if to knit, leave it on the needle.*

Repeat steps between * and * until all stitches are off the needles. If the stitches are too loose, start from the first stitch, and work across and tighten to match surrounding stitches. Bring the tail to the inside and fasten off.

knitwise Slipping a stitch, as if to knit. The two needles are side by side, and you insert tip into the new stitch from below.

long-tail cast on A good basic cast on. See also page 9.

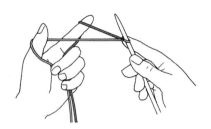

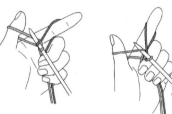

oz ounce(s)

p purl

p2tog Purl 2 stitches together.

place marker Place a stitch marker on the needle. On the next row, simply move the stitch marker over to the right-hand needle and proceed.

purlwise Slipping a stitch, as if to purl. Needles form a continuous line to pass the stitch from one needle to the other.

reverse stockinette stitch Purl the right side and knit the wrong side.

RS right side

slip 1 To move a stitch from one needle to the other needle without knitting or purling it. The stitch is usually moved purlwise unless specified; for example, in ssk, the stitches are always slipped knitwise. See page 14.

slip stitch (crochet) Insert the crochet hook as specified in the project, wrap the yarn around the hook, and draw a loop through to the front. Pull a second loop through to the front and then through the stitch on the hook in one motion. Repeat as needed.

ssk slip, slip, knit these 2 stitches together — 1 stitch decreased

stockinette stitch The right side of the work is knitted, while the wrong side is purled.

tbl through back loop

weave in ends Using a yarn needle, stitch the ends of the yarn back and forth as neatly as possible on the wrong side. Do not knot and cut.

WS wrong side

wyif with yarn in front

yd(s) yard(s)

yo yarn over

Page numbers in *italics* indicate photographs and tables.

Acknowledgments

Thanks to so many wonderful generous people who helped me make this book a reality. To Gwen Steege, who gave me the breathtaking news that my book had been accepted; my editor, Pam Thompson; my technical editor, Charlotte Quiggle, who walked me the rest of the way; and the team at Storey Publishing that made my book a thing of beauty.

Thanks to Sarah Bradberry (knitting-and.com) for her very kind permission to use her Garter Stripe Chevron stitch for my Winter Delights socks.

Thanks to my sample knitters: Virginia Tullock, of FatCatKnits.com, for Wrapped in Hugs (a hand-dyed version), Carpentry Squares, and Touch Me Not; Debbie Doty, for the adult Green Leaves of Summer socks; and Linda Hemmerich, for an earlier version of the Carpentry Squares.

The women I think of as my test-lab knitters comprised some of my earliest "test subjects" and gave me the best feedback and inspired me to actually write this book. Some have provided valuable insights even as this book was going through editing. Without all their assistance this book would not be a reality. Dawn Staring, Debbie Doty, Deborah Ackerman and her daughter Samantha, Edith Walrath, Elaine Sperbeck, Hannah W. Dillon, Jessica Geurriero-Sorensen, Kim Hergert, Laura Senator, Linda Hemmerich, Rebecca Ingersoll, and Stephanie Proulx, I humbly thank you all for your help, encouragement, and affection. I love you all.

And most especially, thanks to Ginny Tullock — you are the one who never let me doubt myself.